A BEGINNING MANUAL
FOR PSYCHOTHERAPISTS

A BEGINNING MANUAL FOR PSYCHOTHERAPISTS

Second Edition

Ernest Kramer, Ph.D.

Professor of Psychology
University of Detroit
Detroit, Michigan

GRUNE & STRATTON
A Subsidiary of Harcourt Brace Jovanovich, Publishers
New York   San Francisco   London

Library of Congress Cataloging in Publication Data
Kramer, Ernest.
    A beginning manual for psychotherapists.

    Bibliography: p.
    Includes index.
    1. Psychotherapy. I. Title.
RC480.K68   1978   616.8'914   78-13510
ISBN 0-8089-1120-1

Grune & Stratton, Inc.
111 Fifth Avenue
New York, New York 10003

Distributed in the United Kingdom by
Academic Press, Inc. (London) Ltd.
24/28 Oval Road, London NW 1

Library of Congress Catalog Number 78-13510
International Standard Book Number 0-8089-1120-1

Printed in the United States of America

CONTENTS

PREFACE TO THE
SECOND EDITION

It is eight years since the first edition of this book was published. I have (like most professors) used my own book in teaching. I reread it once more in preparation for this revision. The main direction still felt right to me, but I found much that I wanted to change. One apparently small change which feels important to me is the substitution of the word "client" for the word "patient." As I note in Chapter 2, I have come to realize that the term "patient" has implications for interpersonal power. It is a word that can now typically indicate a one-down position. I have tried in this rewriting of the book to be generally more sensitive to the power relationships and implications of psychotherapy.

I was somewhat afraid to give a careful rereading to the chapter now titled "The Necessary Client Perceptions for Therapeutic Personality Change." It was the very heart of the book for me, and I was relieved to find that it still represented what feels to me most important about psychotherapy. But the wording at times seemed stiff and even unclear, and I have rewritten it thoroughly for this edition. I have also presented in the appendix to this edition a research method for exploring the implications of the therapy approach described in that chapter.

In some areas I did discover new things that I wished to say. The opening and closing sections of the chapter on technique are quite different from the first edition. My comments on the issues of diagnosis, transference, and the importance of exploring the past are also quite different here. I believe I have grown in my experience and understanding of a number of issues in psychotherapy. As always, I am deeply grateful to the clients who shared and facilitated this growth in me even as I was trying to offer them my help. These changes in me are represented in various changes, small and large, throughout the text.

There is one entirely new chapter in this edition. That is the example of client and therapist at work in Chapter 15. It is a complete transcript of one session of psychotherapy. It seems to me to illustrate and make vivid some of what I wish to say in a way that the short excerpts throughout the book do not. I want to express here my special thanks to the client who was willing to share of herself in print in this way.

Writing in 1978, I am aware of the problem of what to do with the general pronoun: He/she? He and she? change mechanically from one chapter to another? I have not found a satisfactory solution. I have handled it differently in different parts of this book. Sometimes I use the male pronoun, sometimes I use the female pronoun, and sometimes I do use the "he and she" construction. I have used the double pronoun when it seemed to me possible to do so without destroying the force and flow of the sentence. I have probably used the masculine pronoun well over half the time when speaking of the person of the psychotherapist because, frankly, although the sentences were general I typically had myself in mind. I have used the female pronoun at times to give some balance to my excessive use of "he" and "him." I hope the mixture does not appear too clumsy. I hope it will stand as a reminder that we are still struggling in English for a set of nonsexist pronouns which can involve each of us and demean no one.

Ernest Kramer, Ph.D.

1

An Introduction and a Short Story

This is a book about the intensely emotional experience called psychotherapy. It is a book about one person trying to help another deal with disabling confusion and mental pain. I have written it primarily, though not exclusively, for the beginning professional helper. I picture him or her as having spent much time already thinking and learning about the problems of human personality—the average and the exceptional. His or her current professional affiliation may lie in clinical psychology, as does mine, or it may be in medicine, social work, pastoral psychology, or any field where one tries to help a troubled person through talking and listening. He or she is probably working under the guidance of an experienced supervisor or consultant. I have tried to write a book which can be a supplement and accompaniment to that guidance.

I have also tried to write a book that can be read on its own. I believe that psychotherapy, seen clearly, is so important and fascinating an activity that any professional and any layman will find things of interest here. Finally, I also hope to be offering some new ways of looking at psychotherapy to two groups who have had extensive contact with it: experienced therapists and experienced clients.

The approach presented here is, naturally, consistent with my own personal experience as a psychotherapist; there is no other way for a psychotherapist to write a true and honest book on the subject. But, partly because I am also a producer and consumer of research, I have not trusted my experience alone. My approach to psychotherapy has been shaped not only by the many hours which clients and I have shared together, by the theories I have read, and by the vicarious experiences I have tried to absorb through the writings of other therapists, but also by the growing and impressive literature on psychotherapy research. There is no comprehensive coverage of the research included here, but references to selected research investigations appear throughout the book.

Not all the answers have been found. The psychotherapist who presumes to help another human being may not stop safely at the borders of scientifically gathered and tested knowledge. Neither, it seems to me, can he or she safely ignore the fact that such knowledge exists. Many elements of the approach to psychotherapy presented here seem to me to be well supported by the weight of available research; none of them seems to be contradicted by it. Almost all of them are at least potentially open to research investigation.

Most of the principles I have set down here seem to me necessary ingredients of good psychotherapy, although they may not always be the sufficient ones. The stress here on the therapist-client relationship (or, more exactly, on the client's perception of it) represents a major trend in both theory and research in psychotherapy today. It is not merely the focus of Rogers' person-centered approach (Rogers, 1951, 1947, 1959, 1961, 1977) or the writings of humanistic psychologists such as Jourard (1964, 1968), Maslow (1962), and Bugenthal (1966). It is an emphasis which is increasingly felt in almost all approaches to psychotherapy. As one psychotherapist with a predominantly Freudian orientation has put it, ". . . all psychotherapy works (or should work) toward what we shall call a 'Rogerian relationship'" (Holland, 1965, p. 25). This common core will, I hope, make the book useful to beginning therapists who work under a variety of supervisors and within a variety of theoretical schemes. Most experienced therapists with whom the beginner works will agree with much of the material presented here, but some will wish to add to it. Of course, all supervisors will add to the book the real experiences of the interaction between supervisor and beginning psychotherapist. No book can replace that.

Because of their current popularity, brief mention should be made here of those learning theory approaches to psychotherapy which have come to be called the Behavior Therapies. The currently available research has not proved them to be as widely applicable and effective as their most enthusiastic supporters might hope; nevertheless, they do seem to be of aid with some patients, particularly those with relatively isolated symptom problems (Andrews, 1966; Breger & McGaugh, 1965; Grossberg, 1965). They are not the subject of this text, but I can recommend two books which I have found particularly useful as sources of information about them. These are *The Causes and Cure of Neurosis* by Eysenck and Rachman (1965), and *The Practice of Behavior Therapy* (2nd ed., 1973) by Wolpe. I do want to note, however, that Arnold Lazarus—who apparently coined the term "behavior therapy"—feels that this approach is no longer one that should be isolated as a specific technique or school (Lazarus, 1977). He feels it should be integrated with other modes, such as the relationship model of therapy described in this book.

For the approach to psychotherapy presented here, I owe many debts of gratitude. First and foremost, I believe that all current psychotherapy is indebted, whether the debt is acknowledged or not, to the magnificent work of Sigmund Freud. I have made little direct reference to Freud in this book, and I could take issue with much of psychoanalytic practice. Yet his towering genius seems to me to influence all our attempts to deal with another person's emotional anguish. From among living psychotherapists, I am most grateful to Carl Rogers. His wise writings have influenced me both directly and indirectly—through the theory-building, practice, and research which other psychologists have done following his lead. Sometimes it has been my own experiences which seem to have led me by my personal route toward similar conclusions to his. When this has happened, and I have then discovered such conclusions in Rogers' published work, I have felt less timid and lonely about what I myself seem to have discovered.

There are other psychologists who have been important to me as well, but in this short introduction I wish to turn now to my clients. For every therapy excerpt printed in this book, I am grateful to the client who took part in it—although I have taken the traditional course of making sure her actual identity is concealed and her privacy preserved. Although they are rarely quoted directly here because I have few recorded tapes from their sessions, the many so-called "schizophrenic patients" whom I saw when I was a state hospital psychologist seem to have played a special part in my growth as a therapist. Perhaps this is because of the special qualities of openness and need which I seemed to find in them.

In all psychotherapy I believe that the client's needs come first. It is not solely a one-way street, however, and my thanks go to all those clients who have shared with me those intense moments when we both seemed to grow. But I think now especially of David, who came to me desperate in his need and determined to make me help him if there was any chance at all that I might do so. He was, therefore, one of my great teachers. It was to David that I dedicated the first edition of this book. I think he would not mind my expanding that dedication now to others who have added in special ways to my own personal growth during the hours we spent in psychotherapy. Though I am not listing them by name here, I know that certain clients have played a special part in actualizing my own abilities to learn and to love.

I am not like a catalyst in a chemical reaction. I do not merely cause change in others while finally coming out personally no different from how I began. My own involvement, which varies in intensity, has taken different forms with various clients. Later in this book, I shall speak in a formal sense about the importance of the therapist's involvement and of prizing his or her client. But, partly as a balance to my more traditional and scientific approach elsewhere, I want to present a kind of short story here. It is my own version of a classical myth. It first appeared in *Voices: Journal of the American Academy of Psychotherapists* (Kramer, 1975). I appreciate that journal's permission to retell it here.

I MISS YOU, GALATEA

[*Pygmalion, the sculptor, fashioned Galatea from stone and fell in love with his own creation. The gods took pity on him, gave life to the stone, and Pygmalion and Galatea lived happily ever after. I am a psychotherapist, and I know a different version of the story.*]

Even as Pygmalion worked away at the resistant mass of stone, the stone itself seemed to guide him. Beneath the stubborn shell of rock crystals lurked the stone's urge toward its own destiny. Of course, the sculptor also had his own ideas. He held back, though, from making them too definite. His sketches and models were purposely vague, and he looked back at them only rarely. As he worked he would suddenly sense a denser layer that guided his chisel to a different angle or a softer stratum that bent his hand to its shaping. He felt he could have forced a form upon the stone, and not a bad one either, if he chose to use his powerful craft that way. But he let the sense of a buried pattern before him lead the way to its own uncovering.

At last it was done. The beauty of the new-shaped Galatea was before him. He saw it and was dazzled by it. He sensed tears of wonder building a pressure behind his eyes, and from his mouth came the words, "I love you." At that sound of his own voice he felt somehow foolish and inappropriate. He tried to master his own muscles, so that the words he spoke next came out far more softly. "And I want you for my own."

Perhaps the gods heard him, even if somewhat imperfectly, but it may also be that they had no role at all in what happened next. The beautiful Galatea was alive—apparently had been alive for at least a little while because she seemed to have sensed some of the sculptor's words. Pygmalion watched her perfect breasts rise, her perfect body fill slightly with air, preparing to speak the words that would come from her perfect mouth. He awaited his reward.

"I thank you," said the beautiful Galatea, "for what you have done for me." He waited and watched. "I know now," she continued, "that I am alive and beautiful, and that it is because of you." She went on: "I love you, too, Pygmalion, and some part of you will be in my heart when I find that other or those others with whom I shall share new love." She turned then and walked from the studio of the sculptor. Pygmalion felt the pressure of his tears break through, but Galatea did not see them as they spilled down his face.

I miss you, Galatea.

2

Psychotherapy:
Definitions and Goals

Most of the psychotherapy discussed in this book involves two persons. One of them is seeking a kind of help from the other. In psychotherapy, the help-seeker is usually called a patient or a client. A number of the major approaches to psychotherapy were first developed by physicians, and the popular use of the term "patient" may reflect this historical fact. It also probably reflects the powerful role of medicine today. Many people picture physicians as being almost magical authority figures. It is largely this image of power that makes me reluctant to use the term "patient" in the helping relationship this book will describe. As later chapters will make clear, it is important that the help-seeker not perceive the help-offerer as a powerful authority figure who is above question. I do not have any ideal term for the help-seeker, but I have chosen to use the word "client" here to distinguish him from someone seeking medical help.

If he does not have medical problems, then what kinds of help is the client seeking when he comes for psychotherapy? In the classical case histories of older books, movies, and out-of-date television programs, people arrive in the therapist's office with strikingly individual and bizarre symptoms. They may come with a paralyzed arm, with an inability to speak, with some dreadful, but highly specific phobia. These situations do occur, but in my experience they account for a minority of the problems that are brought to the therapist.

Most of the clients I see (and the majority of my colleagues seem to have the same experience) come with some sort of painful problem in living in the world with themselves and with others. I do sometimes see clients who have a fear of the dark, or a fear of cats, or a fear of snakes. But it is rare for this to be the major problem. Much more common is someone with a terror of exploding over his own anger, or a desperate fear that he will never be able to love another person. I see persons who come for help because they are all but totally convinced of their own worthlessness, because their experience of living from day to day builds almost unbearable tension in them. Somehow the world in which they see themselves living is constricted in certain ways, or they are constricted in their ability to act within it. These are the "symptoms" that I most commonly hear about when a person comes to me for help. Such problems are hard to put into words. Here, for example, is an excerpt from a first therapy session with a woman about twenty years old.

Client: I don't know exactly where to start, other than to say that obviously if I'm here, there is something bothering me. And, um, I've been thinking of coming in for quite some time and I haven't had the nerve to, and you know, I wasn't quite thinking what I was doing when I finally walked in today. I decided that this was the day I was going to do it.

Therapist: Sounds like it took a real push to get you in here.

C: It did. Mmm, yeah, a real push, um, well, there are many things but I'd say predominantly that I'm very, very unhappy. And, I don't know, it just, a lot of things that are bothering me. I don't know. Maybe if you ask me a question, maybe I could be more specific.

T: There is nothing in particular that stands out for you? Just generally unhappy or . . .

C: Um, there are many things that are going through my mind which I can't exactly de- . . . you know, nail it for you without going into a lot of different things. I have a lot of

trouble communicating with people my own age. I have with-
drawn . . . well, to start with . . .

Whatever the final "push" was that brought her in to see me, it seems to
have been only the most recent link in a chain of things. She will start
trying to make her self, her uniqueness, clear to me with whatever
comes first now. She has not come for any clear, single reason, however,
but because her personal world is a troubled one, and she hopes that
this thing called psychotherapy may help lessen her troubles.

Some persons come because others send them. Often, once they are
sent, they admit that they are experiencing some sort of difficulty. The
difficulties such a client reports may not, however, be the difficulty
which someone else saw in him. In Chapter 7, "The Beginning of
Psychotherapy," I shall give some examples of the importance of listening mainly to the client's description of his difficulties, rather than to
what the person who sent him said.

The other person in the two-person psychotherapy situation is the
help-offerer. I shall generally call him the psychotherapist or therapist.
He may be a clinical psychologist. He may be a psychiatrist or a social
worker or a specially trained nurse. A number of professions are
contributing to the ranks of psychotherapists. But what distinguishes
the help-offerer in psychotherapy is that he tries to aid the help-seeker
by establishing a special kind of dialogue. His main medium of work is
talking and listening. The therapist believes that many troubled persons
can be helped to grow in this way and that he himself possesses certain
skills and abilities which make it likely that he will be of help to most of
the clients he sees. The talking and listening of the therapy dialogue (as
well as the visual acts of communication) are impelled by both thought
and deep emotional feeling. It is important to remember then that
talking involves not only the words spoken but the way they are spoken.
The spoken communications of client and therapist contain more than
just words. The pauses and tempi of speech, and the stresses and
inflections of vocal tone are important in psychotherapy, as they are in
any communication involving attitudes and feelings (Beier, 1966;
Kramer, 1963, 1964). Listening, then, means listening to the melodies of
speech as well as to the lyrics. The question of just what the therapist
does, that is, what sort of talking and listening he engages in, is the
subject of most of this book.

There are varieties of psychotherapy which involve several clients
at one time. These are called group therapy. There is also multiple

therapy which involves more than one therapist at a time, even though there may be only one client. Couple therapy, family therapy and numerous other variations in the numbers of the participants also exist. In all of these, however, one or more persons are coming for help and one or more persons are presuming to offer help. This book will deal primarily with the two-person situation. Furthermore, the person called the client in this book will be someone who is an adolescent or older. Child therapy is an important area, but it is one needing and deserving a book of its own. I shall also not deal in this book with people in the later years of life. I am not sure how different therapy with these persons is, although my personal experience leads me to believe there are some differences. The main limitation here is, however, my experience. While this book draws on available research and published accounts of psychotherapy, its primary source is my own experience as a psychotherapist.

The Goals of Psychotherapy

The client comes to the therapist because he has problems and because these problems are experienced by him as a kind of suffering. It seems to me that if a psychotherapist agrees to enter into a relationship with such an individual in the hope of being of help to him, a primary goal of psychotherapy must be relief of the client's suffering. Most therapists, and most clients, too, for that matter, also feel that it must not be just a fleeting relief or one which involves unpleasant secondary consequences. It may not be relief or problem solving that lasts for a lifetime. Even the best psychotherapy can hardly hope to be a lifelong shield against all the possibilities for anguish which life may hold. But it seems to me that psychotherapy must point to some extent toward the future, as well as operate in the present. Some psychotherapists, particularly those who practice the highly specific therapeutic technique called psychoanalysis, feel that therapy should ideally make enormous and wide-reaching changes in the total personality of the client. Typically, the criteria or goals such therapists set for the success of psychoanalysis are a description of their concept of the ideal and fully functioning person. Perhaps, though, this is true for all psychotherapists. As a therapist, I care strongly about my client, and hope that he will become an ideal, fully functioning person. He and I may disagree, however, about the nature of the ideal man. I try to perceive and honor this disagreement.

My primary goals in psychotherapy are to offer some relief of the suffering with which the client came to me and to help him to grow and change in directions which he chooses and finds desirable. This kind of growth seems to me to be part of the protection against the potential unfortunate consequences of strictly problem-solving techniques. I think the difference between brainwashing and psychotherapy is that the psychotherapist does not choose highly specific future goals for his client's behavior and personality, while the brainwasher does. I do not mean that the psychotherapist is totally without value judgments or that he imposes none of these upon his clients. I believe strongly that individuals should not seriously harm other individuals. If I should find a client of mine developing unalterably in ways which would cause him to do great harm to others, I would probably be forced to terminate my relationship with him. Beyond this, however, there seem to me many different ways a man can be. Incidentally, because our value judgments probably communicate themselves to many clients even when we do not wish them to, my opinion is that the most effective psychotherapist (as opposed to the most effective brainwasher) is someone who is quite undogmatic about the nature of the good life. I suspect, though, that he does have some ideas about it, and that he believes that a better or fuller life is possible for most individuals.

In his *Autobiographical Study*, Freud (1935) wrote that the aim of psychoanalysis was "to replace a symptom by an act of choice." In these terms, "symptom" is the opposite of choice; it is that feeling or action over which we seem to have no control. I do not want to get into an argument here about free will and determinism; at times Freud himself was much more of a determinist than this quotation would suggest. To avoid this area of possibly unanswerable argument, I shall restate this goal of psychotherapy (which I share) as "to maximize the client's experience of choice." The individual who has experienced successful psychotherapy, in these terms, feels a sense of increased control and responsibility. He does not fancy himself to be omnipotent, but he does experience himself and his environment as acting upon each other, rather than his being the passive recipient of forces within and around him. When a client is relieved of a symptom or problem or some kind of mental suffering, it seems to me that he frequently has the sensation of choosing another way of being. Often, however, it is not simply a direct choice to give up a symptom or problem. As my clients and I seem to have experienced it, it is as if the world of possibilities has become somewhat larger. In the world in which he now perceives himself, what formerly was seen by him or by others as a problem no longer has a place. It may change without his specifically thinking about it or focusing on it as he grows in other ways. Here is an example of a woman whose field of choice in academic matters seems to be getting larger. The previous semester, before entering therapy, she had been put on "pro"—on academic probation—because of failing two courses.

C: I'm a dreadful hedonist. I love pleasure. I will drop anything to have a good time. I'll cut a class, you know, or something like that.

T: [*laughs*] I like your version of "anything."

C: Well [*laughs*], that's just an example of it. That's the sort of anything I did last semester when I went on "pro." But now I realize the two things can live together, because suddenly I have been doing my work. I haven't been pushing myself really, but I have got my reading done for my two history courses and for bio. You know, it's good.

T: It's nice to be able to take care of that part of life without a lot of pressure.

C: I don't exactly know why I'm doing it. I don't have a sign up saying "Susan is on pro—she absolutely must study." I'm just sort of doing it on my own.

During psychotherapy some other things have happened to her for which she does feel able to describe the reasons, but the change in her study habits just comes naturally into her world as she experiences it now.

This stress on choosing and on an expanding personal world is characteristic of the phenomenological viewpoint of this book. The consistent emphasis here is concern with the world of the client. I shall try to describe what the therapist does and what the client does from the vantage point of an outside observer, but that is not where I really think psychotherapy takes place. I believe that psychotherapy takes place in the new experiences and new awareness that occur in the dialogue between client and therapist, as the person seeking help begins to discover new possibilities elsewhere in the world. I assume that the significant psychotherapeutic changes take place in that self-in-the-world perception of the client. They take place in those most basic and certain data: existence and personal awareness. I can never really and fully know the absolute nature of the shared, "objective" world. I can, therefore, only experience therapeutic change through a change in my own personal perceived world, and the same must be true for every other individual. The kind of psychotherapy which interests me, then, is that which causes a change in the client's perceived world; a change which brings about a diminution of the suffering which brought him to therapy and which gives him the experience of choosing among a wider range of possibilities in living than he seemed to have before.

I do feel there is an intermediate goal which must be accomplished before the client can fully experience his own act of choosing. This prerequisite goal is to have the sensation of owning one's self, to recognize oneself as the owner of one's actions and experiences. The young man in the following example is struggling even to own his own feelings of dread and fear.

C: Yeah, but the main thing about this is that I want to know whether I'm really feeling it, or just . . . this isn't all unreal by itself. Whether it's me that's feeling it. Do you understand what I mean?
T: No.
C: Whether I'm . . . I'm saying you know, well this is you, you know, no, not even that. I'm saying you shouldn't feel this. That's not even it. Like it's all phoney, like I'm making it up. I'm giving myself an excuse for something. I don't know that, I don't even understand that.

When I do not clearly follow his first statement, I honestly admit that to him. He goes on to try to clarify what he means. It is as if he feels two persons within himself—a complaining speaker and a cynical listener. He is struggling to unify both of these into a single, honest picture of himself.

I believe that the individual in successful psychotherapy comes to say, "My experiences happen within me." He does not say, "They happen to part of me." He says, "I have done this action," not "This action was done by something within me which is not really part of myself." The person comes to recognize that he is a whole individual, a unique individual, and that all his experiences and actions are part of his uniqueness and his wholeness. He then has the experience of choosing actions from among the various possibilities in which his whole person may engage, not from among different parts of himself. It does not eliminate the possibility of making bad choices or of acknowledging that bad choices were made. Bad choices may be the result of poor or inadequate information, an unsuccessful gamble (we all take risks on purpose at times), or of having misunderstood our experiences. Misunderstanding experience, though, is often the result of disowning experiences or disowning part of oneself. Misunderstanding an experience often comes from not focusing clearly and fully on what is happening within you, or of not being able to label it correctly. Misunderstanding may also come from not recognizing that your experience is really something from within you (even though, of course, it is a response to outside forces at the same time). This kind of misunderstanding, this source of bad choosing, should diminish as successful psychotherapy progresses—as what the client does and feels becomes recognized and acknowledged as fully his own.

3

Theories and Attitudes

Theories are most important to have when you can't see what's happening. It would be possible to spell out all the theoretical foundations and implications of hammering a nail, but the technique is quite clear without these. Neither the laws of inertia nor the physiological theories of what make a thumb hurt and swell are really required. One or two observations of the task should be sufficient to convey its basic principles, and one or two errors should be sufficient to suggest to someone that he or she had better learn to keep thumbs out of the way. Whenever cause and effect can apparently be clearly observed and there are not too many different things to consider at once, theory is a kind of luxury.

When, however, there are a great many factors to be considered at once, having a theory is a way of guiding attention to a particular focus. One way of thinking about a theory is as a method of selectively setting aside that information which, by sheer bulk, is just too much to handle in getting to the core of a problem. A good theory is one that has made a good selection. A theory, by focusing attention on fewer factors, should make the relationship among those factors easier to see.

The previous chapter dealt in part with the goals of psychotherapy. Theories of psychotherapy generally concern either what conditions are necessary to achieve these goals or how particular conditions cause these goals to be achieved. That is, they tend to deal either with what has to take place to make psychotherapy work or with how certain conditions manage to make it work. The first kind of theory—the "what" kind—is closer to observation, to the nontheoretical state. It is relatively easy to think of empirical or testable questions which contribute to this kind of theory. For example, if you examined a successful series of psychotherapy cases and compared them with an unsuccessful set (cases in which the goal was not achieved), you could ask: What conditions took place in one series that did not take place in the other?

The second sort of theory—the "how and why" kind—would go on to ask: Why did these conditions make a difference? The scientific answers to this kind of question can never be as certain as the answers to questions which only ask, "What?" Fortunately, in the vital doings of psychotherapy the "Why?" is less important. I sometimes enjoy speculating about why certain conditions in the client–therapist relationship seem to lead to personal growth for the client. I should like to know more about that. But most important for the practicing therapist is the attempt to identify what the factors are which, for whatever reason, seem to be the necessary antecedents to psychotherapeutic growth.

To return, then, to the "What?" kind of question, it might seem that it could easily lead to the technique of doing psychotherapy. If one could determine what kinds of things made the difference, then all that would be required would be to do those things. Unfortunately, this is not quite the case. The problem is one of too much information, of too much detail. If one were to examine a large number of psychotherapy cases as suggested above, each one would be different from the others, sometimes enormously so. There is no automatically right way of deciding which of these differences made the difference, of deciding which variations in therapy were important in achieving the therapy goals.

The major theoretical assumption which underlies this book is: The way the client perceives the psychotherapist and his or her relationship with the psychotherapist is the most important factor in therapeutic personality change.

There is a fair bit of research evidence to support this notion, and I shall present some of it shortly. First, however, I shall point out one of the very unsatisfactory parts of accepting this formulation. It would be most convenient for the psychotherapist if an understanding of the helpful perceptions and attitudes on the part of her client led her directly to a choice of therapy techniques. By "techniques" I mean here a choice of just what responses the therapist should make and what she should require of her client. Unfortunately, no such firm and convenient guide to these choices exists. For example, my experience and the research literature on psychotherapy lead me to believe that it is tremendously important for the client to regard the therapist as someone who treats her with respect as a person. It is quite insufficient, however, to merely tell the client early in the therapy relationship, "I feel true respect toward you." The ways of conveying this respect, of telling it so that it can be truly heard, probably vary considerably from client to client. Fortunately, the situation is not quite hopeless. There are certain general human communication patterns that can be relied upon; some kinds of action and behavior seem to mean about the same thing to everyone. It is also fairly easy to think of things that a respectful therapist would not do; it is not too hard to think of certain kinds of obvious scorn and belittling toward the client which would work against her perceiving any respect being given to her. Also, the general proposition that the client's perceptions are of primary importance does have one major general implication for the therapist: She must work at being an absolutely first-rate listener (and watcher). She must keep herself open and alive to all the cues regarding how the client views the situation they are both in.

I shall list here now the six necessary client perceptions which seem to me to be the essentials of successful psychotherapy. The first two have to do with the openness and the wholeness of the therapist.

1. The therapist is seen by the client as a real and honest person.
2. The therapist is seen by the client as someone who allows the client's emotional needs to take precedence over the therapist's needs during the therapy hour.

The next two have to do with the importance of trying to share a sense of the client's experiences and feelings.

3. The therapist is seen by the client as someone who is continually trying to follow the client's story.

4. The therapist is seen by the client as someone who tries to actively sense and enter into the feeling experiences of the client.

    The last two have to do with caring and respect for the client.

5. The therapist is seen by the client as someone who considers the client worthy of being helped.
6. The therapist is seen by the client as someone who respects the client's right to be the final judge of his or her own feelings and experiences.

All six of these will be further defined in Chapter 5. Then, two at a time as I have grouped them here, they will be examined in still greater detail in Chapters 8, 9, and 10. In Chapter 6 I offer a provisional "technique" of psychotherapy. But it is a technique which rests upon the client perceptions I have listed. It is those necessary perceptions about which I feel most certain. They are supported by my own experiences and also by the experiences and empirical researches of others. The technique which I then present is not as certainly applicable to all therapy encounters. It is how I seem to be most successful in relating to clients and in making clear to them the helping relationship which I have to offer. I am sure it is far from exclusively applicable to me, but other therapists may find modifications and additions to it useful as they discover the ways in which they can best communicate with their own clients.

Returning to research, it is noticeable in going through the literature that relatively few studies have investigated how the client felt about the psychotherapy which took place. One quite consistent finding from those that did ask this question is that clients tend to evaluate the success of their therapy differently than do their therapists. For example, in a study by Feifel and Eells (1963) the researchers found that therapists judge the success of psychotherapy by the client's freedom from obvious symptoms and an increase in social accommodations. The clients themselves, on the other hand, put the emphasis on changes in inner subjective feelings. Clients and therapists in that study also disagreed as to how helpful results were brought about. While the therapists put their technique first, the clients were more concerned with human, personal qualities. "Patients, in substantial proportion, attribute their assistance to being able to talk with someone about their difficulties in an atmosphere of interest, warmth, and tolerance. In opposing vein, a goodly number of the therapists conceive their aid as issuing strongly from their professional mastery" (Feifel & Eells, 1963, p. 317). Most of the therapists were practicing psychoanalytic therapy, although not full and classical psychoanalysis. Historically (although there have been recent changes), psychoanalysis has stressed the intellectual mastery of certain therapeutic techniques and has assumed that suitable patients will change in desirable directions whenever these techniques are correctly used. This may help to account for the stress these therapists put on their specific techniques during therapy.

Classical psychoanalysis has also put great stress on the client's developing a strong positive attachment to the therapist during certain sections of the analysis. This "transference" reaction is often considered essential for successful therapy. But in a study (Board, 1959) which looked at clients' and physicians' judgments of the outcome of psychotherapy, a client's judgment that her therapy was successful was most likely to be related to the reverse, to whether or not she felt her *therapist* liked *her*. This was strikingly true in those cases where the physician felt therapy had not been a success but the client felt that it had been. In every one of these cases, the client answered "yes" to the question: "Do you feel your therapist liked you?" The client's liking the therapist was, however, also important. Of the eighty-eight clients in the study, not one considered therapy to be successful if she did not like the therapist or feel liked by her. As in the study by Feifel and Eells, here again the clients who felt they had had successful therapy equated success with being able to express their problems and feelings in an atmosphere of interest and understanding, while unsuccessful therapy was mainly associated with a lack of interest on the part of the therapist.

Another study (Strupp, Wallach, & Wogan, 1964) sent out extensive questionnaires to forty-four former clients and their psychotherapists. They found no demonstrable statistical relationship between the outcome of the therapy and how long it had gone on or how intensely the therapist felt it had operated. The authors felt that they could make a distinction in the clients' questionnaire responses between "technical interventions" and "personality characteristics" of the therapist. Although the technique may have been important to the therapist, it was not what most impressed the person who sought and experienced help. "Clearly, what most impressed our respondents was the therapists' personality and attitudes" (p. 23). The major factor they discovered was "the patient's conviction that he has the therapist's respect." Apparently, this respect must come from a therapist whom the client perceives as being real and honest.

> This faith in the integrity of the therapist as a person may be called the capstone of a successful therapeutic relationship subsuming other characteristics. Technical skill on the part of the therapist may go a long way to capitalize on such a relationship, although the present data do not specifically inform us how such a relationship comes into being, is deepened, and turned to maximum therapeutic advantage. However, there is little doubt that a relationship having these qualities represents the most basic ingredient of beneficial therapeutic influence irrespective of the formal aspects of the setting. (p. 37)

The phrase "formal aspects of the setting" seems to refer to what we ordinarily speak of as the technique of psychotherapy. Thus, technique takes a second place. But even though technique may not be able to directly produce warmth and respect, it still seems possible that, to some extent, techniques can be learned which may help us to make our warmth and respect clear and visible to the client.

A more recent study (Sloan, Staples, Cristol, Yorkston, & Whipple, 1975) compared psychoanalytic psychotherapy with behavior therapy and gave further support to the importance of how the client views the therapy relationship. In that study, ratings of warmth and genuineness made by raters who listened to tapes of the therapy showed no relationship to outcome. But ratings made by clients, themselves, told a different story. "For both psychotherapy and behavior therapy groups, there was a strong tendency for patients who reported greater nonpossessive warmth, genuineness, and accurate empathy to show more improvement" (Sloan, et al., 1975, p. 223). I find this particularly interesting since it also applied to behavior therapy whose proponents rarely mention such relationship variables at all. One of the exceptions to that tendency among behavior therapists is Arnold Lazarus. Lazarus gathered data from 112 persons he had previously seen in therapy (Lazarus, 1971). Among the questions he asked these largely successful cases was how they would describe him. "On the adjective checklist the words that were used to describe me more often than any others were sensitive, gentle, and honest" (Lazarus, 1971, p. 19). Perhaps it was partly this finding that eventually led Lazarus, who originally coined the term "behavior therapy," to decide that identifying "behavior therapy" as a particular approach is no longer useful (Lazarus, 1977).

The following excerpt from a therapy session between myself and a man of about twenty illustrates one aspect of the issue of respect for a client. He is talking about a friend who is also in therapy. His description of the friend's therapist may not be accurate, but it does clarify one attitude that can be produced when the therapist's respect for a client's individuality is missing.

C: I was talking to this kid, the guy I met at the bowling alley. He said that stuff about emptiness, you know, and I told him I knew how he felt, and I said that if he had any problems, you know, he should come here. He said that he was seeing somebody, and it was under that guy's *advisement,* and everything that guy told him, he did. And I just [*laughs*], I didn't say anything to him, but I just sort of jumped out of my pants. You know, wow, what a way to live. And it just . . .

T: Man, like that's really being nothing, being told that this is your life at every turn.

C: Yeah.

T: Sometimes you come in here, and you want me to give you answers.

C: Yeah, I know.

T: But boy, if I told you what to do all the time, you'd really know there wasn't anything to you.

C: Wow, yeah, you know, I just . . . It would be like having this little box with you and just saying, "Well, should I do this, like should I park my car here?" [*laughs*]. Press the button and it tells you, you must park two spaces down. You know, if you had something going like that, you'd get so mad, and you'd just throw it away.

The imaginary box—and perhaps that real therapist—tells you directly just what to do, and it tells you indirectly that you are not enough of a person to decide for yourself. Looking over this therapy excerpt now, I think to myself that if you did have the conviction and strength to throw the box away, you'd be all right. But not every client is that fortunate.

Back to the world of theories, there are theories of personality and development as well as theories of psychotherapy. It seems to me that the therapist often has use for a theory of human personality. These are theories about the complex ways in which human beings react to other persons and to the world around them, about how our individual differences develop and interact. Such theories may help the therapist with new ways of trying to understand the client's communications. Like other theories, these are also useful as a way of discarding, obscuring, superfluous information. Out of the unmanageable riches of human personality, they try to select and group the key elements. If the selective focus that remains is helpful, good. If it seems to lead nowhere, then important information has been thrown away and it is time to take a new approach to understanding. Freud's psychoanalytic theory of personality (which is not the same as the psychoanalytic technique of treatment) is one of the most extensive and powerful conceptual schemes for looking at human personality and development (see, for example, Freud, 1927; Rapaport, 1960). Carl Rogers has extended his own theory of therapy into a theory of personality which is also a useful way of trying to understand human behavior and feeling (Rogers, 1959). Various learning theories also offer approaches (for example, Dollard & Miller, 1950; Bandura & Walters, 1963). Theories about personality, about the nature of humanness and being, are not, of course, limited to psychology. In the individual psychotherapy hour, struggling to understand the facts and feelings of the person across from me, I sometimes find my knowledge of Dostoyevsky to be as important as my knowledge of Freud. My main point here is that the theories I try out in a therapy hour are aimed at helping my own understanding of the client. They are not a framework that I insist the client use to understand herself. If my theory of personality forces the client into a set mold, or for that matter makes her distant from my understanding because she will not fit into my mold, then that theory is at that moment a failure.

One of the great occasional rewards of doing psychotherapy comes when a former client shares with you something of what the therapy has meant to her or him. Here is part of a letter I received from a man in his twenties whom I first saw when he was a patient in a state hospital. He had been there for about two years and had already made much movement along that unfortunate path which leads from the active admission wards of the hospital to those back wards where even custodial care is minimal. The letter was written several months after his discharge from the hospital. It reflects some of his doubts and concerns as well as his hopes and gains, but it seems to me to be a letter from a man who has found some extra room to grow in. I put it at the end of this chapter because it is so consistent with the kind of client attitudes I have tried to describe.

>   To begin with, I would like to wholeheartedly and sincerely thank you for your efforts in working through my problems with me. True, I don't sound very enthusiastic now, but we both know if some psy-

chotherapist hadn't worked with me at the time you did, I would still be in the hospital. The words "thank you for your efforts" alone don't signify much meaning. So you'll just have to take my word for it that there is much emotion behind my words. Anyway, to summarize what I've been trying to say is that I'm very grateful for the faith you had in me as a patient and your undying hope for a favorable prognosis in spite of the circumstances at the hospital. In short, these feelings you transmitted to me contributed to my recovery (improvement might be a more appropriate word). [*There are some details about his current situation, and he closes the letter with:*] Well that's about it. Just thought you'd like to be informed. I would enjoy hearing from you at your convenience.

Your friend, Steve.

4

The Setting: Place, Money, and Time

Furnishings

As for the minimum requirements for the psychotherapist's office, two chairs are the only essential equipment. I shall discuss these chairs for a while here because they may help clarify some of my general feelings about therapy. It is nice if they are comfortable chairs; it is nice to have an attractive carpet; and it is convenient to have a desk with its own chair separate from the others. Two chairs, though, are the necessary and sufficient conditions. If you have been in an analyst's office, or simply seen the popular representation of one in cartoons or on television, you will notice that I have omitted the mention of a couch. Whatever special benefit a couch may provide for the highly specific form of therapy known as psychoanalysis, it does not play any part in most psychotherapy. It certainly does not have a role in the kind of psychotherapy described in this book. The technical reasons for its use in analysis can be discovered from many of the standard psychoanalytic works. One rather nontechnical reason which Freud himself gave was that he could not bear being stared at for eight or more hours per day, and his seated position behind the couch placed him safely out of sight. It must, unfortunately, be tempting to stay relatively free of any active interaction once you are out of sight. As we know, however, from accounts by Freud's patients (although not so much from Freud's own accounts of analysis), the founder of psychoanalysis talked a great deal during sessions, and this might have helped compensate for his invisibility.

Because a sharing relationship and respect for the client are important elements in the kind of psychotherapy described here, the two chairs should ideally offer the same degree of comfort. The roles of therapist and client are different from each other, but the differences which operate in good psychotherapy do not include any that justify one of them having a better chair than the other. I may feel that I have special rights, since I might have to sit for a few hours at a stretch while any particular client needs to sit for only one. The client, however, might not as readily grant me this benefit; more probably, he would simply not notice. I think the more likely tendency for a therapist who owns an undemocratic pair of chairs is to automatically give the more comfortable one to the client. I may feel like the gracious and giving host as I stand beside my small, hard-seated chair, and generously gesture to the client to seat himself in the large, over-stuffed armchair across from me. My experience leads me to believe that the client typically does not see it the same way. He is more likely to perceive it as a concession to his weakness and needs, rather than a tribute to my fine hospitality. Democracy in seating arrangements is, of course, often beyond the therapist's control. Not everyone furnishes his own office, and the institution you work in may provide only one comfortable chair (if that many) per office. In such cases, it is usually possible to offer a client a choice of the chairs available. Unless one of the only two chairs in the room is obviously a desk chair, and thus the property of the office's regular occupant, it is possible to place the chairs so that the client does have a choice.

A note about the client's choice of chairs and your response to it seems to fit in here, although it relates to the issues of first interviews which are dealt with in Chapter 7. His choice of where to sit is probably determined by factors in his perception of himself and of you. If the client seems to be trying to shrink into the tiniest and farthest corner of the large seat cushion, if he sits timidly at the very edge of the chair, if he obsequiously sits himself down on a hard and miserable looking bit of furniture while letting you have the only comfortable chair, it probably does reflect one small aspect of the shyness or even dread with which a person may enter his first psychotherapy session. But offering him a choice of chairs should be a way of helping him through this initial anxiety and onto other matters, not a diagnostic test whose results you will then present to him. In other words, it is most probably an error to open an early session of therapy with an interpretation of why the client sits where he does. To fix a client with a beady and inquisitive stare and announce challengingly, "I see you have taken the smallest chair in the office. What do you think that means?" is to do a cold and harmful caricature of the kind of psychotherapist whose real counterpart I wish did not exist. I hope this terribly obvious example will stress the importance of not interpreting and commenting on everything.

To get back to furniture rather than to what one says about it, it should be possible to keep the desk (presuming you have one) from standing between you and the client. I don't interpret choice of chairs to the client, but I am going to risk interpreting the choice of chairs to you. If you manage it so that you are on one side of the desk and the client is clearly on the other, then I suspect you want considerable distance between the two of you. I am not sure what the distance means to you. Maybe there is a question of fear, maybe it is a question of status, maybe it is a question of trying to hide yourself behind a professional role. This last notion seems the most likely to me, and it runs counter both to my feelings and to the relevant research about the importance of the client perceiving the therapist as someone who is willing to be his own real self. If a desk chair and one other chair are all that are available to you, arrange the desk so that the client can at least sit to your side; then you do not need to look across a whole expanse of furniture to see each other.

Two chairs are the bare minimum requirement. I find it almost as important to have in the office Kleenex, ashtrays, and matches. This also suggests a small table on which to put them. Clients do sometimes cry in good psychotherapy, no matter how much the tight social conventions of the world outside your office have tried to teach them that sad feelings should always be hidden. Being able to offer them a tissue is a good way of saving them the embarrassment of sitting through an hour with a wet face and a runny nose. I have had a couple of clients who suspiciously eyed the box of tissues and asked if it was there because they were expected to cry. I have answered, "That's certainly not a requirement here, but I also don't require here that you not cry."

As with tissues, I feel it is a courtesy to provide an ashtray. I smoke a pipe, myself, and I have no objection to the smoke from a client's pipe or cigarette or cigar. Many persons, however, are increasingly conscious of the potential health hazards of smoking. A client, for example, may find my favorite tobacco quite noxious. I pass by my pipe for that client's session. I can manage without it for a while, and I can even resist the temptation (to which I am yielding here) to point out that the strong evidence is all against *cigarette* smoking. What if you are a therapist who finds it hard to tolerate your client's smoke? You had better, I think, judge just how strong your objection is. If you can manage honestly to set your objections aside, I recommend doing so. But if it is a major issue for you, I am sure it is more therapeutic to require that your client not smoke than to continually resent him or her for doing so. I have heard some therapists argue, by the way, that clients should not be allowed to smoke because it will dissipate the useful anxiety that should go into the psychotherapeutic work. I can see the theoretical reasoning for this, but my experience leads me to believe that it just doesn't work out that way.

Some states require that your certification or license be displayed on the wall. Aside from such legal requirements, I see nothing necessarily good or bad about a wall covered with diplomas, a large photograph of Freud, a large photograph of Pavlov, or even a sampler that says "Home Sweet Home." The furnishings and the trimmings, the pictures I may choose to put up on the wall, are a natural part of me. I am not afraid to show something of myself to the client that way, and if I were I might just as well be afraid to have him see my face or hear my voice. The absence of any such trimmings makes an office seem rather bare and cold to me. That is my particular taste, however, and my experience leads me to believe that such furnishing details are much less important to the client. Perhaps that is because he is in the office only during the time when we are there together. During that time, the most important things in the office are overwhelmingly ourselves, with our thoughts and feeling and memories, and the words and behavior with which we show them. If either he or I begin to notice and comment extensively on the office furnishings and wall hangings, it is either an indirect way of speaking about other thoughts and feelings or a sign that the intensity of our therapy conversation has given way to a kind of social chit-chat which neither of us has to come to a therapy office to find.

Fees

Most psychotherapists make all or much of their livelihood from doing psychotherapy. This requires that they be paid. This seems a very simple fact, but it often makes not only the client but also the psychotherapist somewhat uncomfortable. One author has entitled his book on psychotherapy, *Psychotherapy: The Purchase of Friendship* (Schofield, 1964). There is some truth in that, and the idea of friendship or love being purchased is one with unpleasant and somewhat improper connotations. A doctoral dissertation done with me by Dr. Janice Quintal suggests strongly, however, that the client views the therapist quite differently than she perceives even her best friend. We confide in therapists for different reasons than those which help us decide how much to share with a friend. That still leaves the practical question of how we should decide the amount the client has to pay. What is our personal brand of therapy worth, and should we bill the client according to how much good therapy we give in a particular hour? In a clinic setting where fees are highly variable, I once asked a client if she would like to decide how much she should pay for her psychotherapy sessions. She misunderstood me in just this manner, assuming that I meant that it might be a different rate for different sessions.

C: I wouldn't like that at all.
T: Why not?
C: Because I would have to say after each session, "Now how much was that worth?"
T: No, not after each session. That's a horrible notion, isn't it? [*laughs*] I don't think I could stand to find out what I got sometimes.
C: No, because then I would be valuing you, and I wouldn't like that.
T: No.
C: I'd be saying, "He's worth three and a half dollars," and I wouldn't like that.
T: My better clients consider me a $3.98 therapist, but I don't like to boast.

What I really charge for is not the value or benefit that I give to a client. It is for the amount of my time that I give to him. It is my constant intention during the time I spend with the client to be of help to him, and my fee for a given unit of time remains constant. The size of my fee is determined by the particular local, social standards for psychotherapy fees and by my particular evaluation of myself and my experience. In an institutional setting, such as a mental hygiene clinic, the fees are usually set by the institution. To determine the size of your private asking fee, it is a good idea to inquire as to what psychotherapists in your community are charging (even though this should not be the sole determinant of your rates). I have read a few discussions of fees in other books, but I have never seen a discussion that stated any particular figure. I can sympathize with this; it is clearly a matter of the rapidly changing mores of our financial and psychotherapeutic folkways, together with a desire to avoid making some obvious error in print. Despite this, I am always faintly dissatisfied at its omission— perhaps because of my fondness for concrete detail. In this year of 1977, in the Detroit area, the modal fee for relatively young clinical psychologists in private practice is about $40 per session. A major factor in establishing that fee has been the rates described by some of the major insurance carriers. In fact, it is hard to find a lower fee except in special low-cost clinics.

Despite the fact that it is time, and not services, which is sold, I do not charge all of my clients the same fee. I try to be honest with myself about my need to make part of my living through fees, but I do lower my standard rate at times. Sometimes I will have a sense that I am the "right" therapist for a potential client, that I have something special to offer in terms of approach or experience. Or, sometimes the client is presenting a particular kind of problem which particularly arouses my interest. I am most likely to reduce my fee at such times for clients who cannot afford my regular rate. At other times I am more likely to refer the prospective client to a therapist who charges less or to a low-cost clinic.

How Long and How Often?

A psychotherapy session is frequently referred to as a therapy "hour." It rarely is an hour. Until recently 50 minutes was the most popular length of time. The 10 minutes remaining in the clock hour were the therapist's time for brief note-taking and for a few moments of thought and relaxation before another scheduled client might arrive. It has now become popular in some circles to offer a 45-minute "hour" and schedule clients continuously, with no time between. Although I can see the financial advantages of this, I can find nothing else to be said in favor of it. It not only allows no time for the therapist to consolidate his notes or be by himself, but it demands an almost instantaneous cutting off of a client who attempts to complete a thought beyond his 45-minute time limit. And while that somewhat miserly 45-minute "hour" has been increasing in popularity, some therapists now offer a 40-minute "hour." Neither of these shrinkages from the older 50-minute norm ever seems to be accompanied by a reduction in fee.

Although having to stop a client with scarcely more than a minute's tolerance on either side can be a bad thing, I feel that general time limits do have a useful function. A client of mine put it well. She is not, unfortunately, free from general therapeutic propaganda; she is a nurse and probably heard about the importance of limits in her classes. I do believe, though, that her discussion of time limits is something drawn from her real experience as well.

C: You have to be realistic about a situation. That there are times and there aren't times, and we have this amount of time together, and I think if you let it go out of bounds too much then it's really no good in the end. I'm not saying any person has to be so inflexible and rigid and brittle about . . . like one minute after the time, "I don't want to hear from you any more," but you do have other things to do, you have other . . . I mean, you know, it is the same thing in the hospital to tell a patient, "I can spend 15 minutes with you." I don't know how to describe it, really, but I do think you have to be realistic, and if you are unrealistic it doesn't do the other person any good really. I don't think. What do you think about that?

T: I find myself a little confused. In a way it sounds as if you are excusing me for something; telling me you understand it, even though it's kind of too bad. Except that somehow I get the feeling, too, that you sort of welcome these limits being imposed, that some-how you are saying you'd feel more nervous if you didn't have a guarantee that after a certain amount of time I'd say "Leave."

C: That's right. I think I would. That's right. I never thought of that, but that's it exactly. Because if all of a sudden you simply stood up, you know, stood up to show me the time was up, I would think, "Now what did I say then?" Or, "he has gotten disgusted with me." But with the limits set up in advance it's a little easier.

T: You know I'm standing up because of the time and not because of the last nasty comment you made.

C: [*laughs*] That's right. That's called setting limits.

She sees that the time limits protect her in this way. Their very artificiality saves her from the error of judging everything in terms of herself or of what she has just done.

Limits have their function, and allowing the therapist a little time to himself has a function, but the particular length of a therapy session is quite arbitrary. I generally have 50-minute sessions, but this is as much a nod to convention as anything else. In hospital settings, I have frequently had shorter sessions—half an hour or even twenty minutes—where it was convenient for the client to come often and where no time was used up by him in transportation to and from the session (except for the short time walking between his ward and my office). I have also scheduled hour-and-a-half or two-hour psychotherapy sessions, most commonly for someone who, due to his schedule or mine, was able to see me only once a week and found that 50 minutes was not nearly enough time for what he wanted to say.

As these comments have suggested, the frequency of sessions also varies from client to client. I believe I have never seen a client less often than once per week in the beginning stages of therapy, but I have often seen clients at rarer intervals later in therapy. I will talk about some aspects of this later, in the chapter on the concluding stages of therapy. In hospital settings, I have sometimes seen a client four or five times a week. In-patient life in a psychiatric hospital is a strange version of existence, and even the conventions of a psychotherapy session may be more like life on the outside. My experience has led me to believe, however, that for clients who are not in a hospital there is rarely any point to more than two sessions per week. I sometimes make an exception to this for periods of particular and intense crisis, but more than two sessions per week seems to me to interfere with the business of living. There is much to life besides psychotherapy, and if the intense moments of living which take place in the therapy relationship occur too often they tend to sap the energy from other aspects of the client's life.

5

The Necessary Client
Perceptions for
Therapeutic
Personality Change

In 1957, Carl Rogers wrote a now classic paper entitled "The Necessary and Sufficient Conditions for Therapeutic Personality Change." The last of his "conditions" was that the qualities provided by the therapist should be to some extent perceived by the client. As I noted in Chapter 2, since good psychotherapy aims at growth within the client, it is only the things which he or she perceives that can aid in this growth. An increasing number of therapists of various theoretical persuasions have come to agree about the importance of the kinds of conditions and relationships which Rogers wrote of, though some have ignored the fact that they must be perceived by the client. It is within the client's phenomenological world that they must operate. Rogers himself, by the way, did not miss the point. He later wrote "It is also worth noting that it is the way in which his (the therapist's) attitudes and procedures are perceived which makes a difference to the client, and that it is this perception which is crucial" (Rogers, 1961, p. 44).

The conditions listed in this chapter are all phrased in terms of the client's perception. They may not always be the sufficient conditions for therapeutic change, although I believe in most cases they are. They do seem to me to be necessary conditions for change in two-person psychotherapy. They are drawn from my own experiences and the experiences of colleagues and clients, as well as from various research findings in the psychotherapy literature. I shall point out where they overlap with the conditions that Rogers has described. This overlap is encouraging to me, because it reassures me that such experiences of psychotherapy are not idiosyncratic to me. I am sure, of course, that Rogers' writing had some influence on me, helping me to some extent to guide and classify what I felt. Yet I find, looking backward through memories and notes and tape recordings, that I began doing this kind of therapy at a time when my conscious loyalties in theory and technique were to quite a different school of psychotherapy. I also know that I, as a person, have grown up through quite different life experiences and attitudes than those which Rogers has described in his autobiographical writings (Rogers, 1961, 1967). If my personal learnings have led me in similar directions to Rogers, the difference in our backgrounds suggests more strongly that these directions may be part of general human interaction as expressed in the intense interchange of psychotherapy. I remember, in fact, presenting some of my new ways of viewing psychotherapy to a group of therapists in Berkeley, California, shortly after I had received my doctorate. I was, I felt, getting some good results with state hospital patients, with "schizophrenics," and the fact that these therapists had invited me to talk about a different topic didn't seem to stop me from sharing my new therapy approach. One of the group, Gerald Goodman, had recently gotten his doctorate under Carl Rogers. He listened awhile, and then said, "Why, that's what Carl has been teaching us; that's what we've been doing with Carl." With my even fresher doctorate under my belt I told him that he must be mistaken. "I heard all about Rogers in graduate school," I assured him, "and what I'm saying isn't like that client-centered stuff at all!" I was wrong.

In the chapters which follow I shall provide examples of how these client perceptions of psychotherapy seem to operate in the actual therapy situation. In Chapters 8, 9, and 10, I shall also give selected examples of research supporting their importance. That research is drawn from the work of others. I have also developed a research instrument of my own, a "Client Perception Questionnaire" (CPQ), for studying their importance. The appendix to this book includes the CPQ and describes some of the completed research using it. I have already listed in Chapter 3 my impression of the six necessary client perceptions for therapeutic personality change. Here I shall try to give a short definition of each so that it will be easier to follow them in action in the chapters to come.

1. The therapist is seen by the client as a real and honest person. The therapist is not seen as hiding behind put-on roles or defenses or professionalism. The therapist tries to be that self which he or she truly is. This is what Rogers has called the necessary "congruence" of the therapist. The therapist is accurately aware of his or her own experiences and is willing to have those clearly seen by the client. It might, I suppose, be possible for a superlative actor to convey this impression to the client for a limited period of time. But I strongly believe that only a genuinely honest therapist can convey this picture throughout the intense and extended relationship of psychotherapy. Without this real and apparent honesty, no warmth or acceptance the therapist may have to offer can be regarded as valuable. Of what worth are the kind words of someone who seems not to mean them? The therapist is not seen as someone who takes on a special helping role; such an assumed role has dehumanizing elements in it. Rather, the therapist *is* the helper. When the client perceives the therapist in this way, the experience seems to be that there are two real people in the therapy room. The client never feels fully alone there. When the therapist is not experienced this way, the client's sense of isolation increases. Therapy becomes one more painful time of feeling estranged and alone.

2. The therapist is seen by the client as someone who allows the client's emotional needs to take precedence over the therapist's needs during the therapy hour. The therapist's self-awareness and willingness to communicate it are there to facilitate the growth of the client. As enormously important as the realness and honesty of the therapist are, they are never demonstrated for their own sake. The therapist is not seen as someone who talks about his or her own personal life when this could not serve any need of the client's. The therapist is not self-indulgent on the job. When the client experiences his or her needs coming first, the therapy situation beomes one two-person situation in which there need not be a contest for being heard. When this perception of the therapist is missing, a frequent client reaction is, "How come my therapist talks so much about himself during my therapy hour?" This kind of reaction does not seem to me to be related to how much the therapist talks or even to how much the therapist talks about his or her own personal concerns. It is a matter of *why* the therapist is talking. Whose needs are being met?

3. The therapist is seen by the client as someone who is continually trying to follow the client's story. I have tried to word this "perception" of the therapist to emphasize following the "plot" or story content of what the client has to say. The accompanying feelings are, of course, of great importance, but they are not everything. Feelings do not occur in a vacuum; they have a setting and context. I remember a therapy student who was telling me about a client he was seeing. "I really sensed how she felt about Bill," he told me. "I sensed her love and her fear and what an awful struggle it was for her to live with that contrast," he said. "But," he went on, "I couldn't for the life of me remember who Bill was!" The helping therapist is not seen as someone who only listens to the sounds of feeling and ignores the story. He or she pays attention to both the tune and the lyrics. The attempt to follow the story may not, however, always be successful. I believe that the *attempt* to follow is far more important than the achievement, so long as the achievement sometimes occurs. When the therapist's comments reflect a clear and accurate understanding of what the client has been saying, the client will know that there is someone present who has really been listening hard and well. But even when the therapist's attempts to follow are temporarily unsuccessful, the effort can move things forward. If the therapist's comments really reveal a constant intent to follow the story, plus at least some success in doing so, the client will not react to misunderstandings by giving up. In my experience, the client will react by trying to be clearer, to increase the therapist's understanding of the story. It is only in the face of a therapist who makes little effort to follow that a client despairs over his or her ability to narrate the events of his or her own life (or, in the case of stronger and more fortunate clients, concludes that the therapist is hopelessly dense).

4. The therapist is seen by the client as someone who tries to actively sense and enter into the feeling experiences of the client. In this way, the therapist is seen as going beyond the facts of the client's story. The therapist is viewed as someone who hears the client's feelings and who is willing to experience them emphatically. Roger's definition of empathy in therapy fits well for me here. He describes it as sensing "the client's private world as if it were your own, but without ever losing the 'as if' quality . . . To sense the client's anger, fear, or confusion, without getting bound up in it. . . ."(Rogers, 1961, p. 284). When I sense a client's fear, for example, I have an emotional experience of my own. I have a feeling awareness of that fear. But I know that the fear is the client's and not mine. I sense that we are, in part, resonating together, but we are still two separate persons. It is partly just because of that separateness that I can enter feelingly into the client's experience without any danger of being overwhelmed by it. This empathic understanding becomes apparent to the client through the therapist's comments or reflections; it is probably also apparent in tone of voice and gesture, in the therapist's nonverbal signs of involvement in the emotional experiences the client expresses. When the therapist's grasp of these experiences fits, the client probably experiences it as someone sharing in feelings which were thought to be unsharable. The client then feels some lessening of that frightening aloneness which intense feelings can bring. As in the effort to follow the client's story, the therapist does not need to always get it right. If the effort and occasional success are there, there is still some sense of someone sharing in the struggle. It seems worthwhile for the client to focus more sharply and work harder at sharing those feeling experiences which are going on.

5. The therapist is seen by the client as someone who considers the client worthy of being helped. The client clearly feels that the therapist considers him or her worthy of the therapist's best time and effort. The client has a sense of mattering to the therapist; the client believes that the therapist really cares. The therapist is not seen as someone who tries to be helpful only because of money or personal needs, such as professional training goals, even though these may also be present. The attitude I have in mind is close to what Rogers has called "unconditional positive regard" (Rogers, 1957). Unfortunately, the word "unconditional" here has given rise to considerable misunderstanding. It is related to the theoretical construct "conditions of worth" which is part of Rogers' theory of personality (Rogers, 1959; Standal, 1975). It was never intended to mean a saint-like ability on the part of the therapist to totally accept and value all things at all times in all persons. As I view this client perception, the key aspect is the therapist's positive regard for the other person in his or her role as client. This is not a debased role but a valued one. The therapist is not the master of one-upmanship, with the client one-down. The client has come for help, and help is respectfully due. The two of them may have different values in the world. But within the therapy interaction, the therapist is seen as giving high regard to the client's wish to be helped and grow. Respect is given to the client's own definition and experience of what growth will mean. The client seems to experience this as a feeling of genuine caring and regard offered by the therapist. Its absence is experienced as a feeling of unworthiness or rejection. Such feelings may lead to anger or to a deepening depression and sense of hopelessness.

6. The therapist is seen by the client as someone who respects the client's right to be the final judge of his or her own feelings and experiences. I believe that no one can ever know my feelings as fully and accurately as I can. Despite my human characteristic of sometimes hiding from myself, no one can be as aware of what is happening inside of me as I, myself, am. And I believe the same to be true for everyone, including every client in psychotherapy. The client is involved in an ongoing world of feelings and experiences and may, in the midst of these feelings, lack the exact words or symbols for them. One important part of the therapist's activities is to suggest ways of labeling or naming or conceiving of these emotional experiences. But only the client can be the final judge of whether the therapist's suggestions fit. If the client disagrees with the therapist's attempted reflections or restatements of the feelings involved, the client is right and the therapist is seen as flexible enough to accept this.

An insecure or authoritarian therapist (or, especially, one who is both) may argue that only the therapist can know the truth of what lies in the psychoanalytic depths of the client's unconscious. Many psychoanalysts have, however, warned that useful interpretation is always of material near to the surface of consciousness. The therapist may sometimes try to give words to an aspect of the client's personal and experienced world which is not currently strongly felt by the client or on which the client has not yet focused. The client's statement that the therapist is wrong may then be due to this premature formulation. This kind of premature statement might be phrased in the language of psychoanalytic psychotherapy as "bad timing of an interpretation," with the abstract correctness of it still maintained. Such "correctness" seems trivial, however, compared to the need for the therapist to be seen as someone who *tries* to be correct about the *foremost* feeling–experiences of that moment. The important correctness for the therapist to aim at is concerned with what the client has just focused on or is just ready to focus on in his or her ongoing personal world, not a general correctness about the overall history and dynamics of some semi-abstract individual. Together with the preceding "client perception," this seems to be experienced by the client as a feeling of genuine respect. As noted in Chapter 3, this feeling of respect seems to stand side by side with the perception of the therapist's congruence or honesty as being the key perceptions of clients who have experienced helpful psychotherapy. The therapist's willingness to abandon a formulation which the client experiences as wrong is, therefore, no less important than the therapist's ability to come up with a correct formulation. It may, in fact, often be more important.

6

Technique—The Therapist's Responses as Sharing

I shall try to describe in this chapter a way of being and responding for the therapist. But I want to stress clearly that psychotherapy does not require a perfect therapist to succeed. Obviously it could not, for therapy and therapist are never perfect. Psychotherapy is a kind of human interaction. It can only be done by human beings—variable human beings who each have their bad days as well as good. I do not always look forward to seeing each client. I do not always succeed in setting aside all of my own depression or anger or fear. But psychotherapy does not depend for its results on the success of every hour. It is a special kind of human relationship, and like all such relationships, is not a moment or an hour or a succession of separate hours. It exists and changes and, hopefully, grows through time.

I have described the client perceptions which I consider necessary for successful therapy. "Technique" is whatever happens in the therapy session which can make these client perceptions possible and available between therapist and client. Technique, then, does not refer to a style of information-gathering or to a way of deciding what a client "is really like." Psychotherapy, as I see it, is not a matter of the therapist's gathering information and analyzing it. It is a relationship between two persons in which the respect and understanding and personal openness from the therapist provide an atmosphere in which the client can come to experience a sense of increased freedom and personal growth. The therapist listens closely, trying to understand and experience something of the client's world, in order to foster this kind of relationship—not in order to figure out "what makes the client tick."

First, as noted earlier, it is necessary to be an absolutely first-rate listener, to listen well and constantly to the client and to yourself. Then you must respond: Technique is really a summary word for all the kinds of responses which a therapist makes. These responses are not, of course, made in isolation. They are part of a relationship, part of a dialogue. They are not only "responses" to what has just been said or what has just happened, they are also stimuli for what comes next. That "stimuli" aspect will not be as explicitly emphasized here, but it is certainly implicit.

My "technique" as I describe and illustrate it in this chapter may be less general than those six client perceptions; parts of it may need some modification as you find your own style of interacting in the therapy situation. It is, however, a beginning guide. It is a way of looking at the therapy interaction which has been meaningful for me and most of my clients. Yet it is not something I often think about anymore while doing psychotherapy. My "technique" is a beginning point, a starting-off place from which I hope spontaneity will develop. A later part of this chapter deals more with that theme.

Within the whole range of possible therapist responses, it seems to me that the most important types of statements or questions can be viewed as one of two types of sharing. The first for me is the therapist's sharing or trying to share in the client's experiencing. The second is the therapist's sharing his own experienced world with the client. By "his own experienced world" I do not usually mean personal information but rather his own impressions and opinions.

My view of response as sharing reflects the importance of the therapist–client relationship as a partnership. Chapter 5 dealt with the client's perception of this partnership; as I wrote there, it is within the client's perception that therapy change must take place. The client's view of the therapy interaction is of course dependent on the responses of his therapist. Discussing the technique of response, I am now dealing with the therapist's view of the therapy relationship. It is from that perception that the therapist's comments arise.

Preliminaries to Sharing—The Call for Feeling

The therapist makes an effort to share in the thought and experiencing of his client and he tries to make clear to the client that this effort of sharing is going on. In terms of the last chapter, this is, of course, related to the importance of the client's perception that the therapist is trying to be with him in thought and feeling. There are some preliminaries, however, before this kind of sharing can go on.

I urge my client to talk about whatever is important to him. I let him or her know that I am not simply interested in knowing about symptoms. His weaknesses and his strengths (and I let it be known that I am interested in both), his conflicts and his successes, will show in many areas—not just the particular problem areas that brought him to psychotherapy. My client need not be certain that what he is saying is important, but it is the personal feeling of importance that I am interested in. In the time he and I have together, we shall try to omit anything that we know is trivial and focus on whatever might be important. This basic orientation is a preliminary to sharing because it helps establish the kind and range of material we shall try to share. It also makes clear that I will trust my client's judgment as to what seems important to him.

Because it is feeling that is shared most intensely, another preliminary is the therapist's "call for feeling." I may place my call after the client has described some past event: "I wonder how you feel when you think about something like that having happened." I will often call for it at "dead spaces" or silences: "I wonder what you're feeling now." The content or "plot" of the client's story is also important, but feelings and emotions have a special role in psychotherapy. For one thing, the client is more likely to be able to use—and to need—help in clarifying or labeling his or her feelings than factual perception. If he or she is not grossly out of contact with perceived reality as most of us see it, she does not need much help in labeling her direct perceptions. Somehow, though, the labels for feeling are taught in more diverse ways to each person; it is here that common grounds for labeling and clarifying need to be established. For example, families vary far less in what they call a "dog" or a "cat" than in what they call "anger" and "love." It is important to see how your use of emotional labels resembles, and differs from, those of the other persons with whom you interact. In psychotherapy, the therapist is more likely to be able to contribute toward an understanding of what the client is feeling than toward what happened to her. What happened to the client happened in the past. The therapist was not there, and he must depend on the client's story. The feeling is happening, or happening again, now. The therapist can offer his hunches about what that feeling is and means, so that the client can test those hunches against her own final judgment of whether or not they are correct. Finally, feelings generalize to a variety of situations. As rich as the range and varieties of feeling are, they are less varied than all the different specific events that can happen. Any learning about feeling is therefore likely to be applicable to a wider range of situations than any learning about one specific bit of behavior.

Before the therapist can try to share in what the client is talking about, he or she must know quite clearly what is being spoken of, what is going on. The therapist needs to ask questions regarding the content of the client's speech whenever she finds that she is not following the content, and that waiting for a sentence or two hasn't helped. That is, the therapist may wait for a very short time to see if the content becomes clearer but she had better not wait too long. Typical problems that need clarifying are confusing plots, confusions in the time sequence of events, and unrecognized names. Incidentally, these questions aimed at clarifying content often lead to other clarifications. Here is such a situation in a therapy session.

C: It's bad enough going home this time. I really don't want to because Steve and his wife will be there.
T: Steve?
C: I just don't want to have to deal with that.
T: I'm sorry. Who is Steve?
C: My brother Steve, my older brother.
T: I remember our talking about your brother who goes to school and lives at home. I didn't realize you had more than one brother.

C: I don't think of Steve as my brother. When I say "my brother" I always mean my younger brother.

I had to clarify my own confusion about who was who to follow what she was saying at the moment. Her response to my questions led to her sharing important information about how she feels toward her two brothers. I find that this frequently happens: My actively trying to understand what the client is saying now leads us to a better understanding of other areas as well.

Just as questions regarding content help the therapist to be recognized as someone who is trying to understand what the client says, the perception of the therapist as someone who wants to enter into the client's experiences is intensified by questions regarding feeling. The "call for feeling" described above is one version of this. One frequent situation is where the therapist thinks the client is feeling something, but he does not know what it is. "I think you're feeling something now," I may say, "but I can't grasp what that feeling is." Such a comment is appropriate only when the therapist truly has no guess as to the feeling involved. Otherwise, it is a violation of the therapist's congruence or honesty. When the therapist does have a definite hunch about the feeling involved, the more appropriate response is the kind of "tentative sharing" described below rather than the fully open-ended question described above.

Sharing the Client's Experience

Tentative sharing still does have something of the air of a question about it, but it involves more active participation than mere questioning. The therapist has a hunch, often a fairly strong one, about the facts or feelings involved, but he does not feel certain. It is hard to give an example in print of this kind of sharing (it will be still more difficult for the definite sharing to be described here) because energy level and tone of voice cannot be clearly indicated on the printed page. In the following therapy example, the client is a man who works as a teacher. My comments are a kind of tentative sharing, although other things may also be going on.

C: You know, usually if I want to do something, you know, I'll go ahead and do it. But last time Judy came along with me, and for the first time in the world, I wanted her to come. I really didn't want to go there alone. That's completely strange.

T: To go where?

C: To the PTA meeting. I just didn't want to, you know.

T: Maybe kind of scared to be alone?

C: I don't know. I'm not too sure. I was thinking about that and I don't know.

T: Maybe that's not it, maybe it's not scaredness but something else in aloneness that you don't have words for yet.

C: Yeah, maybe. Funny, I don't know. It's just a real strange feeling. The only thing I can do is sort of attach it to that emptiness, you know, depression, because . . . I don't know, what else to do with it.

T: Maybe having people around, maybe having Judy around helps keep the nothingness away.

My first question ("To go where?") is simply an attempt to follow the factual content of what he is saying. My other comments, however, are tentative statements of what he may be feeling. He examines these statements. He is tentative, too, as he rejects the first ("scared to be alone") and provisionally accepts my second hunch. This acceptance (his "Yeah, maybe") quickly leads him onward to a further exploration of his own feelings. He and I both begin to feel and see more clearly what he is experiencing.

What I call "definite sharing" takes place when the therapist feels sure what's happening. He or she goes clearly beyond questioning. She states what's there, and perhaps she even advances beyond what's there to move forward and anticipate what might come next. At such moments the therapist moves forward as if she and the client were having the identical experience together and speaking in one voice. This level of strong and definite sharing seems to occur only when strong feelings are involved.

In definite sharing, in the intense sharing of feeling, in which the therapist tries to speak both with and for the client, the therapist strongly feels his own sureness—but he is not above correction. He still knows (as noted in the last of the client perceptions described in the previous chapter) that the client must be the final judge of what is happening. Continuing the therapy session quoted above provides an example of this.

T: Maybe having people around, maybe having Judy around helps keep the nothingness away.

C: Yeah, but then, you know, this has always been the problem. You know, why do I have to . . . have to define my existence on other people? You know, why can't I be just for the sake of being, and let that be that?

T: [*With a sure sense of sharing and moving things forward*] You want closeness, and even when you can have it, when the closeness is there, it gives you a sense of being weak. You don't like having to need it.

C: Um, no. Not so much that as . . . it's not the being weak, the closeness for the sake of closeness. Not for me saying, "I'm me because I see myself through other people, through my relationship with A and B and C," but I am just, you know, I'm not one. I can't take myself and, you know, just be. Because there just doesn't seem to be anything there . . . except for the . . . do you understand?

T: [*With a hunch just beginning to form, but admitting his own confusion and fallibility*] I'm not sure.

C: I don't see myself as anything but a bunch of relationships. And this is the important thing, and my . . . and my real . . .

T: [*With a somewhat tentative sharing*] It's kind of worse than a sense of being weak.

C: Yeah, it's . . .

T: [*Definite sharing*] Like you're really doubting your own existence if there's not anyone else there.

C: Yeah. I think about things, like, if, if nobody else is there: then what am I, what's the use of me?

T: [*Strong definite sharing*] What's the use of an empty shell, of emptiness? Why should it take up space? It's not even real.

C: There is none.

I began my attempt at sharing here somewhat tentatively. I then moved quickly to a kind of definite sharing. The client disagreed with that attempt at sharing, with that interpretation of his experience. I accepted this, admitting my unsureness in the situation. I was then able to move to a new attempt at definite sharing, and this time it was one which rang true to the client's experiencing.

This sharing of feeling seems most important to me when the client is experiencing some emotion or beginning to re-experience a feeling, but has not yet given clear and vivid wording to the feeling involved. The therapist's sharing response is a heightened statement of what the client seems to be experiencing. The therapist's wording, tone, and energy level are, therefore, important. The highest level of all of these occurs for "definite sharing," because that is honestly a higher experiencing level for the therapist.

The Therapist's Experiences—Self, Interpretation, and Advice

The therapist not only tries to share in the thoughts and experiencing of the client, but he makes an effort to share his own thoughts and experiencing for whatever gains the client may be able to draw from them. Of course, the kind of sharing in the client's world described above must also—as in any meaningful dialogue—involve a sharing of the therapist's own experience. Rogers (1961) and Gendlin (1967), writing within a person-centered framework, have clearly seen this. The further descriptions below of the kinds of personal sharing the therapist does may help to clarify the difference between his sharing in the client's experiencing and his sharing of his own experience with the client. First, though, a similarity: As with his attempts to share in the client's experience, the therapist shares his own experiencing as vividly and clearly as possible.

One kind of experience the therapist shares is his own personally experienced response to what is taking place. The emphasis here is on feeling responses, rather than cognitive or thinking responses alone. Frequently there are direct emotional responses to the client, to what he has just shared with the therapist. The client in the example below is a professional woman who is planning to move out of her parents' house into a place of her own. Until this session she has showed much mixed feeling about the move—so mixed, in fact, that she seems to have done nothing about it. Finally, her plans have taken shape.

C: It will be hard, but I have got to go sometime anyway.
T: When are you going to make the move?
C: Well, tomorrow I'm going to . . . I think I found some rooms, and I can't see these rooms today, but tomorrow or Wednesday I'm going to. I really am.
T: You're stepping fast. It sounds good!

It seemed meaningful both to our relationship and to her honest recognition of her own feeling that I was willing and able to genuinely share the enthusiasm. If it is a strong and honest response the therapist may well greet some plans of the client with "that's great!" He may also honestly say at times "I get angry when I hear that." The therapist's respect for the client does not require that the therapist value every act of the client's. It seems to me that true respect more nearly requires that the therapist be open with his reactions when their values differ. Conversely, the therapist should also be unafraid of sharing strong, caring feelings. There are moments in the lives of some troubled clients where it is life-giving for the therapist to be able to honestly respond by saying, "I care, I care whether you live or die."

In such comments, the therapist is disclosing a real, and often an important, part of himself. Among psychotherapists, Jourard (1964, 1968) has been particularly active in urging self-disclosure as an important activity for the psychotherapist. For him, this does not mean only letting reactions and feelings show; it often involves specific statements about the therapist's past or present behavior and experiencing. In a research study, Powell (1968) showed that self-disclosing statements from the therapist caused the client to make both more positive and more negative statements about himself. In other words, the therapist's openness leads to greater openness from the client. It seems to me that the danger here is of transgressing the second of the client perceptions listed in the previous chapter: that the client feel that his needs come first during the therapy hour. The therapist's self-disclosure should be elicited by the therapy interaction, and should be something from which the client might draw a meaning. Its aim is to serve needs of the client, not the therapist. The self-disclosing statements in Powell's study were all very short ones. This brevity probably helped to serve a therapeutic purpose without impeding the flow of therapeutic dialogue.

A therapist's interpretation of a client's statements is also a kind of sharing of the therapist's experience. "Interpretation" is sometimes used very generally to mean almost all of the therapist's comments. Some schools of therapy define it as a statement made with "the therapeutic intent of . . . (confronting) the patient with something of himself which he has warded off" (Colby, 1951). In this discussion, however, I use interpretation to mean a statement about *connections*. The connections the therapist is pointing out may be between motivation and action, between events or experiences described at different times in the therapy but apparently showing some important similarities, or (probably most important) between actions and feelings. I offer an interpretation when these connections strike me with sufficient force that it would be dishonest of me to keep them to myself, or when I have the feeling of wanting to share them. I try to be generally open and alert to connections and similarities of this sort; in this way, they come to me. But I do not go specifically seeking for specific connections. In other words, I do not see it as the primary business of the therapist to go hunting for interpretations. The therapist should not, I think, go actively hunting for any particular kind of comment or way of looking at things. I hope to have an open-ended kind of listening, plus a knowledge and involvement in human personality, that makes me alert both to feelings and to these sorts of connections in what the client is saying. When I think I notice such connections, how forcefully they strike me is my main gauge as to whether or not they might be useful to my client.

The client in the following excerpt came into therapy partly because of certain compulsive rituals. There were various apparently meaningless acts which he felt he had to perform. He referred to these as his "magic," and in a previous hour he had made some connections between this "magic" and certain kinds of religious feeling. He is talking now about his grammar and high school experiences in a Catholic parochial school.

C: I think even if I went to public school, I would have been the same way to a certain extent, but I know that there's not that freedom you have in public school. You know, you just sit in class and . . . you know, you just sit there and whatever the teacher said you used to copy down notes religiously, you . . .

T: "Religiously!"

C: [*Starts to see the connection between his school behavior and his "magic" religious rituals.*] Right [*laughs*]. I guess that fits pretty well.

T: Because, somehow, in the school you went to, acting the way the teachers wanted you to meant acting religiously.

C: Right. Everything. I guess I was doing the "magic" then. Everything was more or less superstitious religion, the whole thing was.

Here, I suggested the connection between his religious school behavior and his present symptoms in my single word comment, "religiously," though I expanded this a bit later to be sure he and I were looking at it the same way.

A special class of interpretation is the "interpretation of resistance." In traditional terms, this means that the client is somehow resisting getting down to the business at hand. My own experience of it is that sometimes during therapy the topic seems to have shifted from an apparently important, personal matter to something of noticeably less importance. A shift in topic to something which seems at least as important is likely to be a sign that there was some meaning in the previous topic which I had missed, and that meaning has become the overt focus of our talking now. It is only when I feel that the importance level, or sometimes the intensity, of what we are talking about has gone down that I find the notion of "resistance" at all useful. My "interpretation of resistance" is my comment on this drop in level of importance or significance of topic. If I have a hunch as to why it occurs, I will offer that guess to the client for us to look at together. Otherwise, we will start fresh to look for the reasons together. Early in the therapy session from which the following excerpt was taken, the client had been talking about her fears of marriage and the difficulty of having a truly meaningful marriage. Then somehow, somewhere, she had quickly shifted the topic and tone.

> C: And I also kind of feel that, as a political system, democracy is dead. No political system can last for ever. It isn't good for ever. Because people are not the same for ever, and people are politics. That is my current view of political philosophy.
>
> T: I think you are playing it cool today.
>
> C: I don't know whether I am or not. I am trying not to get hung up in things. I think that was another thing last week. I wanted to run away from talking to you.

It may, by the way, be argued that this talk of politics ("people are not the same forever") was a metaphor for the earlier theme of marriage worries. It would not have been wrong to suggest that possibility, open-mindedly, to the client. Here, though, I responded to the "cool" tone with which she pronounced her political philosophy, in contrast to her previous more involved manner. She was then reminded of an attempt to "run away" from our interaction.

Although discussions of political philosophy are often digressions from the important business of therapy, personal philosophies certainly do play a part. One kind of sharing that the therapist engages in is sharing his or her opinions and views of how things are. Usually, in such situations, I share something of my view about the nature of feelings and how feelings are. My suggestion, direct or implied, is that the client give my view or opinion a provisional try in the chance he might find something of value for him in it. Here, for example, are two opinions about the nature of feeling which have value for me and have apparently been of value to some of my clients.

1. *A person has a right to have and recognize his or her true feelings even when the circumstances of life operate against that feeling being linked to action.* This sort of "need" to be honest with yourself about your honest feelings is important even when it is your own choices of behavior that keep you from being able to turn those feelings directly into action. In either case, whether the circumstances are something you have chosen or are the result of forces from outside you, I think it is better to have honest feelings despite helplessness, than to have helplessness and lie to yourself in addition. I tend to take issue with any client who tells me that he will not have a certain feeling because there is no use in having it.

2. *Opposite feelings do not contradict, do not deny each other.* I am not just talking about what textbooks call schizophrenic ambivalence; I find that, for anyone, opposite feelings may be opposites but are not necessarily contraries. I can love and hate. You can be sad and happy. We can have both feelings at the same time, and we have the right to maintain both.

In addition to offering opinions, I think that a good therapist does sometimes offer advice. I think of this as divided into goals–advice and means–advice. Goals–advice is advice about how and where things are to end up. I do not particularly mean in the long-range sense, not advice about the great and eventual goals of life. I am thinking about answers to specific questions which clients ask their therapists. "Should I marry him?" Should I really take this job?" When I have a strong feeling about the appropriate goal or action for a client, I share it. But I do so with an honest tentativeness that acknowledges that these are my goals and that therapy does not depend upon the client agreeing with them. I acknowledge that my particular values enter into this—as they do, and I try to point this out in many of my statements. The client is not required to accept these values. They are there, linked with the goals and actions that I find implicit in them, for him or her to examine and choose or reject. I realize that the idea of offering advice runs counter to the common concept of the therapist's role. That common concept might say: The therapist himself is value-free and, at least in his job as therapist, he has no set of values or life-philosophy which he should offer. My own feeling is that the congruent and honest therapist is a person, a real person, with his own set of values based on the real experiences of his own life. If he tries to deny this to the client and himself, he may end up only by conveying them in a subtle, self-deceiving, and often distorted way. When my values, including goal-related values, seem relevant to my client's situation, it is part of my honesty as a therapist to share this honestly. I am probably fortunate, as a therapist, in the fact that I am virtually never sure that my own values are perfectly right for any other person. Beside the fact that I urge my client to consider them freely, my own tentativeness about their general applicability helps me to share them in a way that leaves clients free to reject them.

What I call means–advice has to do with ways to goals. The goals in this case may have been described by me or by the client. I may make specific suggesions about how to try to accomplish specific tasks, or I may make more general statements about ways of accomplishing practical or emotional goals. For example, if a client who seems interested in changing things tends to concentrate too much on past impediments to change, I share my opinion that it is much more useful and important to try to initiate new behavior than to try to understand how old, maladaptive behavior was caused and maintained. I suggest that we can, if necessary, try to deal with what seems to stand in his way *after* he actively tries to be different. This may seem like a basic principle of therapy which I should impose on all my clients. I find, however, that some clients to whom I offer this advice still insist upon understanding the blocks to new behavior before they will give it a try. If a client continues to maintain this attitude, I trust this judgment he has made about himself and his needs, and we try to operate along the line he has suggested.

The final kind of therapist sharing I am going to describe here has to do with the therapist's admissions of his or her own imperfection and fallibility. I let the client know very clearly that I make mistakes. In fact, I am fairly often in the position to let him know concretely that I have made one. I sometimes realize during the therapy hour that I have been dense about a previous comment of his, or that I have led him off the track of something important. I share with him my opinion that I have made such an error and invite him to let us go back and try to rectify it. In the session from which I quoted above, where the client was discussing parochial school and religious magic, I somehow led off in another direction well before he had deeply explored the meaningfulness of the topic. Obligingly, the client followed my bad lead and did make some interesting observations on the new topic.

T: That is interesting, but I feel that I led you off the track today. You were talking about how the business of your background in parochial school worked into this business of self-assertion.

C: That's right. Even when I first came to college everything was . . . this was when I was very unhappy, when I first came and was really, really unhappy . . . well, you're on your own, but that didn't bother me at first.

The readiness and obvious ease with which he returned to his earlier train of thought seemed to confirm my guess that I have diverted him from unfinished business.

I also share with a client if I find I have been inaccurate in communicating my own feelings. Although I try to be honest, such situations do occur. Sometimes the client notices them first. If I am accused of being inaccurate in my statement of my own feelings, I try to examine them again, whether or not I tend to agree immediately. If I think I have or may have been inaccurate, I share this feeling with the client; of course, if I think he is wrong in his accusation I share that too. In the next chapter, I shall deal with the importance of training a client to take issue with and disagree with his therapist.

Return to "Go"

I remember reading somewhere in a paper by Carl Rogers that he had been listening to tape-recordings of various therapists. At certain points in each tape, he felt he could clearly hear the "technique" or special approach for which each therapist was famous—even on his own recordings. And, reflecting on that experience, he felt that those moments when the therapist's special technique was most obvious were the worst ones in the therapy. The meaning I draw from that is that "technique" may be helpful, but spontaneity is better. I have in mind a kind of informed spontaneity, a spontaneity marked by attention and respect and caring. I think it is that kind of spontaneous openness that grows in good therapists over the years of experience. What, then, is the role of "technique"? It is, for me, a place to go back to when I feel lost. Remember the "GO" space on the Monopoly board? Sometimes the instructions send you back there to begin again. When I feel lost or confused or adrift in my interaction with the client, I return to GO. That is where I make myself remember my technique, my provisional "rules" for doing therapy. But I do not stay there. It gives me the structure and tentative rules I need to start out again. As in Monopoly, the GO space is not a stopping point but a place from which to step out again. I try to move out once more into the informed spontaneity of the human therapy interaction. Perhaps I shall move further along this time. Or perhaps only a few steps. But when I feel the need to return to GO once more—and that feeling will come—it will be to rest there for just the time I need. And once more to make a new beginning.

Note-Taking

Some brief comments on taking notes seem appropriate for the conclusion of a chapter on technique. Note-taking during the therapy session seems to me to be distracting to both the therapist and the client. Only an unusually poor memory seems to me a sufficient excuse to take notes during the session. Frequently, I take notes immediately after a session. How much or how little I write down varies. To me, the most important thing to write down (at least in terms of my own memory) is what I call the "cast list." I try to jot down the names of the significant persons the client has mentioned during the previous hour, together with a phrase about each to help me remember who he or she is.

Tape-recording a therapy session gets all of it down in a permanent form without the therapist having to do any writing. I have found it extremely rare for clients to offer any objections to tape-recording or to show even nonverbal signs of being bothered by it after a few minutes. It is more often a distraction to the therapist, although he or she can learn to overcome it. One problem with tape-recording is that some therapists may take the security of having an hour on tape as an excuse for not personally remembering what took place. In such cases, suddenly discovering that the recorder didn't work that hour produces a desperate feeling. Another problem with recording an entire session on tape is that it takes just as much time to listen to a tape as to record it.

The usual point of note-taking is to be able to look quickly at a brief statement which will remind you of what you want to know. The chief value of tape-recording is for therapy supervision or for the therapist's self-teaching. It is extremely valuable for these purposes because it is such a complete record; it even includes the parts that you would otherwise find easiest and most pleasant to forget.

7

The Beginning of Psychotherapy

The psychotherapy relationship begins, in a sense, as soon as either you or the client hears the other's name. Most typically, the client hears of you first. Your first real interaction is likely to come on the telephone when he or she calls to make an appointment with you. I try to make it clear to the client that the appointment we set up together commits us to only one meeting. I tell her, "Let's get together and see how it works out. Let's see if it looks like I could be of help to you." The first meeting—as I will probably try to clarify later when I see her in person—is our chance to interview each other. We shall decide together if psychotherapy, and psychotherapy with me, is worth trying.

Usually, the appointment is made for the first available time convenient for both of us. Sometimes, however, I seem to hear a special urgency in the voice on the other end of the telephone. It may show up particularly just after I have suggested an appointment which is several days away. To my ears this special sound is not just a tone of disappointment in not getting an earlier appointment, but it has a note of panic in it. I do not like to inconvenience myself, but my commitment to trying to help others creates certain responsibilities. I may not be sure that the urgency I hear is really there, but I am in a profession where I often urge other people to take action without having to be certain. Therefore, when I think I hear this note of panic, I quickly re-examine and rethink my schedule and offer the person the nearest possible appointment. I may say something like, "Look, it sounds to me like you are really feeling the pressure. I can make time on Tuesday at 1 o'clock. Let's get together then and see what goes." If she tries to reassure me that she needs no such special treatment and can well wait until the first appointment I suggested, I may let her talk me into it. But I have to be the judge of that. I must also remember that my offering her an earlier appointment does not require her to present urgent problems when she comes.

The First Session

I noted the name of my prospective client when the appointment was made, and when she first comes to the office I greet her by name. It is my way of reassuring her that she has come to the right place and that she is expected. Next I share with her any information about her that I may have. Often there is nothing to share other than what she has already told me on the telephone. Sometimes however, another professional person, or a friend of the client, or a relative, has taken some part in making the referral. This sharing of whatever information I may possess sets the stage for the sharing that we shall do together later on. I have, of course, a responsibility to any professional person who refers a client to me. I try to be sure to tell the referring physician, for example, that I find it important to share with the client whatever information she may give me.

In addition to helping establish the framework of honesty and sharing in which I wish to work, this initial sharing of information helps us to locate any mistakes we may have about why we are getting together. One source of such error can be the professional who has referred the client. I remember an adolescent boy who was sent to me via another psychotherapist. This therapist did not want to undertake the treatment himself because he was a personal friend of the client's family. He told me that the boy had a school learning problem, and that the boy's physician felt that psychological factors must be involved.

> T: What's your best subject in school, Tim?
>
> C: English, I guess. I like to read and things like that.
>
> T: [*Trying to identify where the areas of school failure are*] What's your worst subject?
>
> C: Math.
>
> T: I guess you do pretty badly at things like math.
>
> C: I guess. So far, I've always gotten at least an 85 in it, but it's not as good as my other subjects.

At this point I realized I had been misled. Eighty-five is not a failing grade. Regrettably, I was well into the interview before I got this information. Had I told the boy immediately that he had been referred because of school difficulties, I would immediately have learned that he had none. It was later revealed that the boy was seeing a physician for severe stomach trouble and was referred to a psychologist because no organic basis could be found. I could have discovered this quickly had I allowed the boy to discuss it. I often find that clients are quickly able to reveal important things about themselves if allowed to do so. I have also learned that well trained, well meaning professionals may give a very misleading picture of the person you are to see.

Another source of error in first meetings comes from what the client has been told about you and about how you are to help her. This is especially important when the client is a child. Both parents and school authorities often find themselves at a loss to explain to a child why they feel she should see a psychologist, and their ways of solving this problem may be strange. I recall an early example of a ten-year-old boy who was sent to me for psychological testing. I naively went on with two hours of various psychological tests before I took the time to really talk with the boy. At that point, he asked me, "Will I make it?" I said I didn't understand, "Am I O.K. to get in?" he insisted. In a few more minutes I finally discovered that the boy thought he was taking these tests as part of an entrance requirement to get into Cub Scout camp. I have remembered since then the importance of discovering why a client, of whatever age, thinks he has come to you.

I generally wait to see if the client makes his own choice of what to say to me first—if he begins speaking. If he is silent, I often ask, "What brings you here?" If the picture I begin to get is one of long-standing anxieties and problems, I may ask, "But why did you come now? You've been sweating this out for a while now; what finally made you decide to come here now?" I find that this sort of question helps the client to focus on his or her immediate situation and it helps her know where to begin. It is also part of how I structure out interaction, of how I tell her what I expect of a client. It says: I expect you to talk not only about the past, but about what's happening here and now.

I also try to make clear during the session other points about psychotherapy as I see it; some of these are already familiar to you from earlier sections in this book. For example, I try to make clear to the client that psychotherapy is talking and listening about important things. Frequently, I try to find an appropriate place in the first session for stressing the special importance of experiencing and talking about feelings. Some excerpts from a first interview may help to give an idea of how an initial session goes. The client is a woman who had recently changed colleges. She shares with many persons difficulty in communicating her feelings to others. The demands of the psychotherapy situation, of the listening and waiting therapist in front of you, can accentuate such a problem. After talking briefly and generally about her difficulties, she went on:

C: Since I have been at this school, I have noticed this a lot more of myself. I am afraid of people. I'm afraid . . . of . . . communicating. I have a tremendous lack of self-confidence in everything I do, to the point . . . that . . . I'm afraid to enter into anything. Afraid to say anything. I really am.
T: It's a great situation, your problem is you're afraid of people and have trouble communicating, and I expect you to come in, sit down, and tell me all about it.
C: Yeah. [laughs]
T: It's kind of a bind.

I try to sense her immediate feelings and difficulties with me, as well as the problems that brought her to me. I let her know that I realize that facing a psychotherapist can be a painful and awkward experience.

I try to gather the information that the client wants to give me about her current situation. I want this information in order to share in the client's experience, not because I am an information gatherer. I do not try to form a coherent picture of the client's life and then try to discover special meanings in it. My aim is to try to establish a certain kind of relationship with her. My attempts to "understand" are made to help achieve this aim.

I do not have any standard set of interview questions which I feel must be answered by all persons before I can begin to help them. My responsibility to help begins as soon as the client and I are in contact. For that reason, all the material in the previous two chapters of this book bears directly on the first session. I try to begin as soon as possible with the kind of sharing I discussed in the preceding chapter. Perhaps more of this initial session can help give an example of this.

> C: One thing is I have a, a thing about my weight. It affects everything I do. I mean the moment I wake up, I've been on and off diet pills two or three years now . . . and . . . it's just an obsession. Everything I do is centered around how much I weigh today, or, you know, whether or not I put on . . . Like right now, I'm walking around in a coat, and it sounds stupid but it's because, if I wear pants . . . well . . . I always wear a long shirt or coat to cover my rear end, you know, business like this.

> T: [*Trying to clarify my understanding of the client's situation by rephrasing it in terms we can both look at*] One part of you says it's stupid, and the other part can't let go.

> C: I know, right, right. Perhaps another good reason why I am here today is that, within the last two days, the boy that I've been going with for three years, whom I'm supposed to be engaged to, just decided that it's not sure. The whole relationship is going the wrong way. I can't get along with him. He's a man I should be enjoying completely and, planning, you know, life in the future with. We're both unhappy together now, and this doesn't seem right. I know it's my fault, that it's because of the unhappiness I feel and that dissatisfaction with myself that I take out on him. And he doesn't understand enough, to say, you know, "what's wrong with you?" or be able to talk to me about it.

> T: [*Asking for information at first, then making a guess about what's happening*] How much can you talk with him about it? Kind of what you're hoping is, if only he'd ask the questions that would enable you to level with him.

> C: He doesn't. I can't even talk. I'm kind of . . . [*beginning to cry*].

> T: [*Wanting to share in her emotion and communicate my sharing, but recognizing the difficulty in this new situation for her*] Makes you sad to think about it, but you don't know me well enough to show the sadness yet.

C: [*Nods in agreement, and sniffs hard in the fight between wanting to cry and wanting to hold back the tears.*]

T: [*Trying to share in her feeling, but also trying to share my feeling that it's better sometimes to freely communicate yourself and your feelings to others*] I see you're trying to wear a smile like you're trying to wear that coat, to cover something up. And I'm not sure if either is worth it.

C: [*Sniffs*] That's very funny, and there it is, and that's one reason I knew . . . if just the fact that the moment I'd walk through the door here . . . I've never, sat down and talked to anybody really . . . [*sniffs*] . . . who I considered of any authority or anybody who could really help me, who I wanted to unload on, and I knew the moment I walked through here and sat down with you, I . . . it was just going to well up, and you don't even know what it is, you know. This is basically what happens if I do try to talk with him. There are so many things I can't express to him, he wouldn't understand or, that I'd want to make him unhappy with, but I automatically just start crying. It's a very difficult thing. You know, I'm not the type of person that really cries that much, unless perhaps if I'm alone or if I have to. You know, I think about these things, and that's why I get into this terrible depression [*sniffs and sighs*].

T: [*Trying to share in her feeling and trying to show my respect for the whole person that I sense is there*] Got to really go down low. I've sort of got the feeling that part of what you're saying is, you just came in, you're feeling sad, you start to cry. And you want me to know that's not the whole story about you.

C: Yeah, yeah, I know.

T: O.K. Tell me some other things about you. What's good with you?

Even in this first interview, then, I have tried to sense her experience of herself, and I have tried to share my understanding of it with her. In the excerpt above, for example, I tried to share in her experience of sadness. Apparently I was at least partially accurate and successful in this, as her tears showed. Then when she tried to choke back those tears, I tried to share with her my own experience that fake smiles are not worth the work they take to wear.

I have pointed out that the therapist is not primarily an information gatherer, but my last question above illustrates one kind of information I sometimes seek. I try to know more about my clients than just their problems. Therapy and conversations that go on in psychotherapy are about important matters, but it is not only problems that are important. Early in therapy I stress that the good parts of a person are as important and as much a part of her as the problems which led her to seek help.

Just as I try to get my client to help me know her early in therapy, I also try to help her know me. I try to answer briefly but honestly questions about my attitudes toward her and my aims in psychotherapy. I often encourage the client to ask questions so that she knows I am willing to answer them. This encouragement is often necessary because the popular stereotype of the therapist pictures her as all but utterly silent. Occasionally, I find myself having to give a brief, impromptu description of my whole view of psychotherapy. Such a situation came up here.

C: I was going to ask you, what should I expect from you? Because I have never been, you know, I have never gone for any kind of help or anything, and I don't know what sort of thing should evolve or anything.

T: O.K. For a start, in terms of operating procedures, um . . . questions in both directions are fine. Do feel free to ask me . . . I don't have any kind of capsule summary though of how I do psychotherapy, or how it helps . . .

C: [Interrupting] Is this considered psychotherapy?

T: Do you like "counseling" better?

C: Well that's what I was wondering, whether . . . counseling, that's the college catch-all for nobody knows anything.

T: Um, I guess I like psychotherapy as a term a little better than counseling because on a college campus counseling does mean all sorts of things, counseling means . . .

C: [Interrupting] Filling out schedules and . . . yeah.

T: So I dump the term counseling for that reason. But I don't care that much what it's called. I guess it's the business of talking with another person regularly. Somebody who is to some extent an expert at . . . trying to sense how . . . other people feel. It may be providing a somewhat different way of looking at situations than they have. Someone who is willing to be honest and . . . maybe helps you to be more honest with yourself, more honest in the sense that . . . kind of . . . being more in touch with what feelings you have, and when, and what sets them off. I suppose the goal of it, in a way, is to give you more a sense of being in charge of who you are and what you are like. Not to make you any special way, but ideally able to do some choosing in the business.

C: Yeah.

T: And strangely enough that seems to happen fairly often just through the business of talking and listening. I'm not sure why, but I'm glad it does.

C: [*laughs*]

T: It's a strange business. Here's, you know, somebody you don't know at all yet, you're just getting to know, and I obviously, as well as implicitly, put demands on you to be honest, to not only trust me in the sense that you tell me private things, but also to disagree with me when I'm wrong. That means you have to trust the fact that I'm going to put up with that, put up with that disagreement. So if you have any questions that will help you to get to know me in ways that will be useful to you, you ask them.

I let her know my hopes and goals for how we shall be interacting together in therapy. I let her know, too, that I realize it is different from other interactions she has experienced. I suggest, at least implicitly, that it may take some getting used to.

In the comments just given, I tell her that I want her to disagree with me when she thinks I am wrong. This is one of the most important things to establish at the beginning of psychotherapy. I have found it important to encourage my clients to question my opinions. I try early in therapy to make quite specific my invitation to express openly any disagreement with me which they may feel. I first saw this issue as part of the general problem of establishing trust in the therapist. After all, we are not used to telling another person private things about ourselves. It feels risky, perhaps dangerous, to reveal one's self to an unknown other. "What do you need to know in order to be able to trust me?" I sometimes ask of a client. I urge her not to trust me just because I am a professional. "Listen to me, watch me, ask me questions, psyche me out. You probably won't end up completely sure about me, but it will help you to decide how much of a risk you are taking and want to take." And I find that the kind of trust that seems most important is trusting me to accept disagreement. She can tell me intimate things about herself if when I misunderstand them (as I sometimes must), I allow her to set me on the right track again. Then she can trust my respect for her and also can learn to trust her own judgment more and more. (This is clearly related to the last of the six principles described in Chapter 5—the idea that the client is the final expert on his or her own feelings and experiences.)

The client's expressed freedom to disagree openly with me increases my sense of freedom. It gives me a sense of increased permission to offer possibly mistaken hunches or interpretations. Without the freedom to say things that may be wrong, I find I cannot do good therapy. I must be able to express hunches, to share guesses out loud, without having to be certain of them. If I had to be absolutely certain of everything I said to a client, I should become either very timid or very cocky. Neither attitude seems appropriate in a psychotherapist.

Practical Problems

The practical issues of future meetings and payment are set up in the first therapy interview. There is no set time at which these have to be spoken of. Often the client will raise questions about them, but if she doesn't, it becomes the therapist's responsibility to do so. I am aware that fees, for example, must be discussed during the first hour together. This awareness often sensitizes me to some appropriate place in the conversation for discussing them. If no such "appropriate" place occurs, however, I use the last part of our session to talk about it. I make sure that there are a few minutes left when I can do so. It seems unfair to announce your fees and your available hours when the client has no time to discuss them with you.

So far, I have discussed the client whom I will continue to see in therapy. Sometimes, however, the client and/or I decide that we should not work together. The client may decide that psychotherapy is not what she has been looking for. If her perception of this seems correct to me, I encourage her. She may decide that she wants to see more than one psychotherapist before committing herself to treatment. It is her privilege to do so; perhaps she will find someone with whom she has more rapport. I ask her to call me when she makes her decision. Sometimes the client would like to see me for psychotherapy but she cannot afford my fees. Each psychotherapist must decide when, and to what extent, she is able and willing to adjust her fees. If the problem cannot be worked out, it is important to have a list of low-cost treatment facilities to which you can refer the client.

At times the therapist decides that she and this client should not work together. If it happens that you really dislike or feel severely uncomfortable with a client, it is usually unwise to try to work with her. Of course, these feelings may pass, but there is no guarantee that they will change. One might say to such a client, "I think you're right to be seeking this sort of help now, but I don't feel that you and I, in particular, would work out the best. I just have a sense that I wouldn't be the right therapist for you. Let me give you Dr. X's and Dr. Y's numbers. Give them a call—I'll call them first and see if either of them has a free hour, if you like—and see how things work out with them." In other words, I feel that when such situations occur it is the therapist's responsibility to try to help the client find somewhere else to go. I feel that after this, the therapist should, for her own sake, try to discover the source of the dislike or discomfort she felt with the client. Such situations will, hopefully, grow rarer with the therapist's personal and professional growth.

The Fear of Being Crazy

One other frequent issue which appears early in therapy should be mentioned before this chapter closes. It is not always present, but when it is, it is worth noting even if the signs of it are spoken softly and indirectly. This is the fear of being crazy. Some clients seek therapy because they have a general sense of being troubled; some have specific problems. Some are living with the terrible fear that they may be crazy. Raimy has written about his view of this problem in an interesting book edited by Mahrer (1967) called *The Goals of Psychotherapy*. He finds that it is almost always present: "While seeing both college students and hospitalized adult male veterans, I was struck by one thing they all seemed to have in common: all of them expressed in one way or another a conviction that they might be losing their minds" (Raimy, 1967, p. 120).

If this fear arises and the client asks me "Do you think I'm crazy?" I ask her first, "Tell me what 'crazy' means to you. It means different things to different people, and I can't answer you until I know what you mean by it." I listen very carefully to her definition, and then I try to answer her honestly just as I try to answer her other questions honestly during psychotherapy. It is rare that I think a person is "crazy" even by her own definition. But it sometimes occurs.

I remember a woman whom I had already seen for several sessions. She came into my office one day and told me that she had been reading about schizophrenia in a friend's psychology text. She had listed the symptoms, as they were described there, on a sheet of paper. Then, in a parallel column, she had listed her own symptoms. She pointed out that there was a great deal of overlap in the two lists. She was showing me her definition of "crazy" on that paper. She felt it fitted her, and she wanted to know if I agreed. I told her something like, "All right. That's a pretty good description of your weaknesses, of what's wrong with you. If you want to be labeled just in terms of your weaknesses, then you are schizophrenic. But that list doesn't say anything about your strengths. For all the messes you get into sometimes, you're managing pretty well. You manage to stay in school. You don't have to be hospitalized. You make sense to me in here. Guys do call you for more than one date. So, O.K., you're schizophrenic in terms of your problems, but that's not the whole story about you." I answered her question, her fear, as directly and honestly as I could, but I also reminded her that that was not the whole truth about her.

I tell a client if, by his or her definition, I think he is crazy, but I tell him more than that. I tell him that craziness does not scare me and does not make me pessimistic. It is one more important thing about him, one more thing that we will explore together in the course of psychotherapy. Thus, the terrible word "crazy" can be spoken, but the edge is taken off it. It is not the end of all things, but only one fact at the beginning which is subject to change.

8

The Openness of the Therapist

This chapter and the two that follow will review the six client perceptions listed in Chapter 5. Each of these chapters begins with a restating
of the two client perceptions of the therapist to be dealt with in it. After
discussing the conceptual meaning of them, excerpts from psychotherapy sessions will be given where these perceptions seem to be
operating. Since, however, these are ways in which I believe *the client*
must regard the therapy relationship, I cannot be certain that these
excerpts apply. There will be moments in therapy when it appears to
me, looking back at them, that I was conveying these perceptions to the
client. These examples will be times when, looking back at them now, I
believe I was making clear who I was, my attempts to experience that
other person with me, and so forth. Following these therapy excerpts,
here and in Chapters 9 and 10, I shall give some descriptions of the
findings from controlled research which seem to bear on the material of

the chapter. This will not add up to any thorough review of the research literature, but it will be a selected sampling.

The first of the necessary client perceptions in this chapter is that *the therapist is seen by the client as a real and honest person.* As I noted in Chapter 5, this is similar to what Carl Rogers (1957, 1961) has referred to as "congruence." For him, the therapist who meets this requirement "is freely, deeply, and acceptingly himself, with his actual experience of his feelings and reactions matched by an accurate awareness of these feelings and reactions as they occur and as they change" (Rogers 1961, p. 283). But awareness is not enough. The therapist must be willing to let his own awareness be visible to the client. In fact, in my framework here, it is useful in therapy only if it is perceived by the client; its visibility is a must.

There are two closely related aspects to this reality and honesty of the therapist: one, he is accurately aware of his own experiences, and two, he lets those experiences be seen by the client. Perhaps a better wording for the second aspect is that the therapist does not hide parts of himself from the client. He may, however, ignore some of his own experiences during the therapy hour. He may try to ignore those experiences which intrude on meeting the client's needs. If the therapist is experiencing pains, problems, or pleasures which are quite separate from his interaction with the client, therapy will best progress if he can successfully set these aside. He does not deny their reality, but because they are not the important thing during this hour of interaction with another person, he puts them in a distant second place. *The therapist is seen by the client as someone who allows the client's emotional needs to take precedence over the therapist's needs during the therapy hour.*

If, however, these extraneous intrusions become too strong, or trying to ignore them becomes too all-absorbing a task, acknowledging them clearly becomes important. It seems to me quite appropriate to say at such times to a client, "Some things that happened early in the day really made me damn angry. I want to tell you that, so that you don't notice my angry feelings and feel they're due to you or a reaction to you." Such times should come rarely, but they do come. Often when they do, such acknowledgment of them not only warns the client but makes it easier for the therapist to really set them aside and get down to the task of therapy. On the still rarer occasions when these outside feelings keep intruding, it sometimes becomes appropriate to cancel the therapy hour with appropriate apologies to the client.

Such strong intrusions of my outside feelings into the therapy hour are extraordinarily rare. I can remember only a few occasions in the past several years when I cancelled a session because of these feelings. Something about being intensely with another person in a helping relationship is so absorbing to me that it temporarily shuts out the outside cares which I had a few minutes before. They may still be at the edge of my awareness for the first few minutes of the therapy session, but then they are no longer important. I do not think this is some kind of "denial": my problems are still there when I focus toward them again, willingly or not, after the therapy session is over. I can speak with full confidence only for myself, but my strong belief is that you will also find this effect if you let yourself get strongly involved in the intense helping and sharing role of the therapist.

The second client perception, noted above, is also an injunction against the misuse of the first principle. As I noted in Chapter 5, the therapist is not self-indulgent on the job. He does not demonstrate his openness and wholeness by talking about his own personal problems when these could not possibly serve any need of the client.

To return to the first of the client perceptions listed here, Freud stressed strongly that an honest therapist was essential for analysis.

> The psychoanalytic treatment is founded on truthfulness. A great part of its educative effect and its ethical value lies in this very fact. It is dangerous to depart from this sure foundation. When a man's life has become bound up with the analytic technique, he finds himself at a loss altogether for the lies and the guile which are otherwise indispensable to a physician, and if for once with the best intentions he attempts to use them he is likely to betray himself. Since we demand strict truthfulness from our patients, we jeopardize our whole authority if we let ourselves be caught by them in a departure from the truth. (Freud, 1915, p. 383).

As a therapist, I try to help my client become accurately aware of his own experiences, and I ask him to communicate that awareness clearly and truthfully. As a therapist, I try to set a model for those tasks. I do not cast all my experiences of the day before him, but I do try to be both aware and open about the experiences that arise from our interaction during the therapy hour.

This aspect of the therapist has also been described as "genuineness." "Genuineness implies most basically a direct personal encounter, a meeting on a person-to-person basis without defensiveness or a retreat into facades or roles, and so in this sense an openness experience" (Truax and Carkhuff, 1967, p. 32). As these authors see it, the other essential therapy attributes of empathy and warmth must wait upon genuineness. It is only in the therapist who seems genuine or authentic that empathy and warmth can be valued. Rogers (1961) has also stressed that "congruence" must come first. If the therapist seems unable to trust his own feelings and to trust them to show, he appears untrustworthy to his client. If the therapist is clearly hiding something from himself or from his client, his honesty is open to question. It is reasonable for a client to demand that he trust his own honest feelings only to an honest and trustworthy therapist.

It is hard to provide convincing illustrations of where these qualities of reality and honesty are perceived in a therapist. Because the key element is that of the therapist being a real person, rather than hiding behind a kind of professional role or mask, it takes some experience with the therapist over time to judge this. The client has that experience; the reader of brief, quoted excerpts does not. In the following section from a therapy hour, the client is just beginning to work on trying to know me and trust me. She is trying to decide who is really there with her.

C: It's embarrassing—it really is. My feeling is, you know, what the hell do you care? And how . . . I mean, it's so hard to be a listener. That's one thing I admire in other people. It's a hard thing to be. That is why, I, I couldn't, you can't say things to a lot of people, you know . . .

T: Well, kind of two parts: one is that you feel embarrassed in asking me to be a listener; the other is that it is kind of hard to believe that I *would* be in that sense, because why should anybody bother?

C: Yeah. Right.

T: Well, for what it is worth to you, maybe I could explain a little why I bother. Um, I find that when I'm able to have a relationship with another person that is helpful to him, I get better.

C: Are you sick? [*laughs*]

T: [*Laughs*] Well I'm not sure I'm willing to say you are either.

C: Oh, I don't . . . I'm not willing to say I am either. I just say that, I . . . there are certain things that just, at this time of my life it just feels like, if somebody could listen to . . .

T: Well, you know, I do this for a living too, of course, but I also find it meaningful to me partly because it is a growing experience for me. It is a job that pays off well in a number of ways for me.

I try to show her that her doubts about me are acceptable and that I seriously consider them. The doubt that anyone could seriously listen to her seems real and important. I'm also willing to tell her that therapy is not simply a professional activity for me, but a personal growth experience. I do set that statement, though, in the context of helping her. That is to say, I share with her my perception that it is when I act in a helpful relationship to others that I find myself growing in the psychotherapy interaction. I think I may make my realness clear to her in another way here. I am not willing to call either of us "sick." I do not take an exalted role for myself, nor do I give her a debased role (this also relates to the important client perception of a therapist who respects the role of client—something I shall discuss further in Chapter 10). My last comment to her above looks a bit as if I'm on the verge of violating my second client perception: that the therapist should be seen as someone who lets the client's emotional needs take precedence over the therapy hour. But she apparently understood my earlier comments well enough to not misperceive me as being selfish on this count.

The therapist is frequently demonstrating his own congruence when he shares something of his own personal philosophy or values with the client. I think I most often do this when I suspect that the client and I share some common values, but that the client denies his because of some desire to have an unrealistic, perhaps overly perfect, picture of himself. The young man in the following therapy session is talking about the fact that his chemistry professor never calls on him in class.

> C: He always calls on the same couple of girls that sit in the back who don't know the answers too much, you know? They're not dumb or anything, believe me. There is no one . . . but they just have trouble with chemistry, that's all.
>
> T: There must be some dumb people around.
>
> C: Yeah, well, I knew one girl who was in my French class, and she's not dumb but she just can't do chemistry, you know. Not that I can especially, but she just has a little bit more trouble than I do.
>
> T: That sounds like a little rosier view of people than I have. I hear you say that nobody is dumb. Do you really think that?
>
> C: No, because I know there is one kid in the class who is a real idiot.

This is a client who has learned fairly well to disagree with me. When he has had a different view from mine, he has shared it. I, therefore, feel able to be straightforward about our disagreement here. His last comment above seems to suggest that, as I suspected, it turns out to be less of a disagreement than it initially appeared. My openness about my opinions seemed to lead him into being more open about his. He was able later to discuss more about his earlier insistence that no one could really be dumb.

Being real and honest with a client means being willing to explore honestly where you may have failed him or her. In the therapy excerpt below, the client and I are discussing her previous session. I had had a severe cold and laryngitis. She felt I had wanted to get rid of her, to rush her out of the office. Her complaint is not about that, but about the fact that I suggested she stay at the same time. She is complaining about my inconsistency, my incongruence.

T: Anyway, it seemed to you like I was phonying you last time.

C: Yes, that's the feeling I got.

T: I'm pretty sure that a lot of me wasn't, but I also trust your sensitivity. You know there are two real people in here. We are tuned in to each other. We listen to each other's guesses about what happens, so maybe there was some part of me I wasn't tuned in on last time. Some kind of phonying may have been going on.

C: The way it seemed to me was, you had a cold, you had laryngitis, you weren't feeling too well . . .

T: And all I did . . .

C: You weren't getting anything accomplished, you know. I guess I was moving slowly. I don't know your head, but if I were in your place I would feel kind of badly because nothing was happening and, you know . . .

T: [Remembering having offered her the choice of staying or leaving, and beginning to remember some of the feelings that went with it] I'm squirming because that starts to sound real.

C: And you knew I was down. You didn't want to make it worse by saying "Well, that's all for now" or something like that, so you gave me the option of staying. Yet I don't think you really wanted me to stay.

T: Kind of, I was down because not enough was going on for the time and energy I was putting in. I sort of didn't want to let you know how tired I was, but I wanted you to make it easy on me without my having to be open about it.

C: In a sense, but, like, I guess in a sense I'm too demanding of you . . .

T: Well, you know, I'm so demanding of you in here, Susan, I don't see how that could be too demanding of me. I make hard demands on you. I've got to be ready to meet demands for honesty if I'm going to put such tough ones on you. It's fair play. I tell you to come in here and talk, not just honestly, but talk honestly about stuff that can scare somebody out of their wits.

C: That's true, I guess. Demand is rather a harsh word. It sounds like you were standing over me with a stick saying "Tell the truth, tell the truth." But you are expecting complete honesty of me: expecting it and expecting it.

It seems that in the previous session, I had not been open about problems of mine which did affect our interaction in the therapy hour. Had I told her then that I was feeling tired and sick and having trouble keeping up with what she was saying, I would surely have bothered her less than I did by hiding my feelings. Fortunately, our relationship was good enough so that eventually she was able to discuss these things with me. I may have been a little extreme in my description of how demanding I am of her. She senses this and corrects me. But she does know that I am "expecting . . . and expecting" honesty of her, and I feel she has the right to expect the same of me.

Honesty and openness are not the same thing. I may honestly tell someone that there are certain things about myself which I will not discuss. If I do not try to give him false answers and do not try to convince him I have told him something when in fact I have not, my behavior is still honest. I believe, however, that for a therapist to be seen by his client as a real and honest person, he must have some willingness to be known.

The therapist must, to begin with, avoid misleading the client about his thoughts and feelings. He does not convey a false impression of his total reaction to the client. He lets the client see when certain things that are said in therapy disturb him, and he then tries to use this shared information to make the therapy progress. In addition to this there are times when the therapist's willingness to be known extends to previous things in his own life. I talked about this briefly when I discussed "self-disclosure" in Chapter 6. When the therapist shares with his client experiences of his own which resemble what the client is going through, it seems to make it easier for the client to say more things—both good and bad things—about himself (Powell, 1968). I remember a client of mine, a college student, who had been working toward a career in dancing. Now, toward the end of her college career, she was giving up dancing. Other values and interests had come into her life. The change in goals seemed like an honest and realistic one, but it was certainly an extremely painful one. I had a similar experience in my own past. I told her briefly about my own desire to be a professional singer and what work I had already done before I finally decided on a change of career. She told me that she felt very lucky that I had had such an experience, because she was sure it helped me to understand her. She thanked me for sharing it with her. My sharing seemed to have two main effects. It made it easier for her to talk about her changing values and how she reached her eventual decision on them. It also seemed to make it easier, when I shared with her my remembered pain, to bear the pain she was feeling now.

For me, one powerful advantage of trying to be truly myself as a therapist is that I have access to my own experience and memories. If I am simply a "model therapist," if I am merely a "well-trained psychologist," I may remember no more than what I learned as a psychologist. I may not recall those other parts of my experience which might contribute to my understanding of the client and myself. In the example above, of the student who was giving up dancing, my access to my own experiences in music was helpful to her.

Music is a powerful part of my life; the next example of "openness" of "congruence" deals with it, too. The client is a man in his late twenties who plays percussion and keyboard. It is our third session together, and we are still in the early stages of learning about each other.

> C: I feel it's really easy to lie with words, and it's . . . That's how come, I guess, I like instrumental music. I guess it's, it's harder . . . [*to communicate with instruments than with words*] but at least people are more into reception of it in that way.
>
> T: It's harder to lie, but also easier to stay indecisive.
>
> C: Yeah, well, in a way I agree, and in a way I say, no. Say I am playing a certain rhythm. It's important to be something. There are a lot of things it isn't. So in a way it is a decision. However, it is abstract enough to where someone who, say, disagrees with me about words can find what they like about that or not. And we both have more fluidness in that way . . .

He is a man who does, in fact, use words in ways that are often hard to follow. The metaphors of music help him to express himself. He seems to me to be talking here about the fact that certain kinds of messages, such as a drum rhythm, invite the listener to find an acceptable part more freely than the limiting messages of words. But as we talk, I realize that we have not explored anything about our own backgrounds in music. I want to find out more about his so that I can understand and experience where he is at more accurately. I want him to know about my background in music so that he can better estimate how much he can trust me to follow his when he draws his similies and metaphors from the world of music.

T: Well, I'm not sure where you want to go with this, Hank. I have a sense that we have been talking a lot about music and music as a metaphor. Yet I know very little about what you actually know about music and do in music. And probably the same is true of your knowledge of me.

C: O.K.

T: Do you feel that it's worth exchanging?

C: O.K. [*a sound of warm agreement*] I feel like I know about you . . . You say you had some voice lessons. I can tell by the sound of your voice. You know . . . occasionally some sort of example you use . . . like the tempering of the tuning scale or the reverberation . . . So I kind of infer an ability for you to speak in musical languages.

T: And I kind of assume that you know that language in a technical sense, too. That you read music and that you are technically musical. But I have never checked that out.

C: O.K. I can read music. I'm technically familiar with it, at least.

We continue for a short time to share information about our backgrounds and knowledge. It enriches our ways of being able to speak to each other. Later in the session, for example, I believe he is trying to express something about his efforts toward good communication. He is trying to convey to me that he does not come into a therapy session with a speech all prepared. He tries, rather, to find his words there in front of me—sensing that we thus get better in touch with each other through his very effort to find the way of speaking. But—like some individuals who are labeled "schizophrenic"—he expresses this in a kind of metaphor.

C: One thing I noticed lately from seeing a symphony. They always do their tuning in front of an actual audience, and it's part of the ritual. The concertmaster comes out and gives the concert pitch. Mmmmmmm. It all goes on and, O.K., they're all in tune. See, blues groups don't do that. And rock, they don't do that. It's almost like: Let's see how professional we can be and have all this done in secret and come out and surprise everybody and be in tune. I'm finding out that the concert people [*symphony players*], whether they are conscious of it or not, they are putting themselves in tune with the audience in the process . . .

I do feel that he is sharing an interesting musical observation. But I also strongly believe that he is expressing something about his communication process with me. He is trying to speak of how he puts himself in tune with me and how he lets me be part of the process. My willingness to be open about my understanding of music has, I think, made it easier for him to find a way of communicating with me.

Some Relevant Research

I noted in Chapter 6 that there is research evidence (Powell, 1968) for the fact that self-disclosing statements from the therapist increase the number of both positive and negative self-statements that a client makes. There is also evidence bearing on self-disclosure in a study by Barrett-Lennard (1962). Barrett-Lennard defined the factor he labeled "willingness to be known" as "the degree to which one person is willing to be known as a person, by another, *according to the other's desire for this*" (Barrett-Lennard, 1962, p. 5, italics added). That final phrase relates it to the second of the necessary client perceptions given in this book: the need for the client to see the therapist as one who uses the therapy hour for the client's emotional needs and not his own. Barrett-Lennard found that the client's judgment of the therapist's "willingness to be known" was highly correlated with the client's improvement in therapy as judged by various psychological test scores. There was also a highly significant relationship between the therapist's judgments of client improvement and the therapist's own judgment of his willingness to be known. The therapist seemed to see improvement in those clients with whom he was most willing to share a part of himself.

In addition to his "willingness to be known" factor, Barrett-Lennard also attempted to study four other factors in his research (1962): level of regard, empathic understanding, unconditionality of regard, and congruence. These factors were measured by his Relationship Inventory, a series of 85 statements about the therapy relationship which are given a score for how true they are in the client's particular situation. For example, the statement "He is willing to tell me his own thoughts and feelings when he is sure that I really want to know them" contributes to the score on the "willingness to be known" factor. One reason the study will be referred to frequently here is that Barrett-Lennard's research approach is in agreement with the viewpoint of this book in judging the client's perception of therapy conditions to be of primary importance.

> Although it is not supposed that a client's conscious perceptions would represent with complete accuracy the way he experiences his therapist, it would seem that his own report, given under suitable conditions, would be the most direct and reliable evidence we could get of his actual experience (Barrett-Lennard, 1962, p. 2).

The factor of congruence was found to be related to both the amount of change after five therapy interviews and to improvement at the termination of therapy. In fact, at the end of therapy the client's perception of the amount of congruence his therapist showed was the factor most highly correlated with his improvement.

A later study (Mills & Zytowski, 1967), using some of Barrett-Lennard's original data plus some new data, clarifies the importance of congruence. Scores were examined from four of the subtests of Barrett-Lennard's Relationship Inventory—the tests measuring congruence, empathy, level of regard, and unconditionality of regard. All four of these factors had been found to be related to therapy improvement (Barrett-Lennard, 1962). Mills and Zytowski did a statistical treatment of the scores called a Principle Component Analysis. This factor analytic technique aimed here at discovering whether some general process might be operating which accounted for the change in more than one part of the total Relationship Inventory. They found it was possible to describe statistically a general scale of components which accounted for about two-thirds of all the variance in the four subtests. The particular scale, or subtest, which contributed most to this general component was congruence. In other words, if a high degree of congruence is present in a relationship, then high levels of empathy, level of regard, and unconditionality of regard are likely to be associated with it. The relationship among these four scales is, of course, far from perfect; they do not all go up and down together. Some of the complexities of the relationship will be discussed in Chapter 10, but the main point here is that a statistical analysis tends to support what a theoretical analysis suggested before. An honest, congruent therapist is the most important single factor in a successful therapy relationship.

Additional support for the importance of congruence comes from various studies by Truax (summarized in Truax & Carkhuff, 1967) with what he calls "genuineness." Traux's description of what it should measure resembles closely the descriptions of congruence developed by Rogers and Barrett-Lennard. This concept of genuineness has also been found to be meaningfully related to progress in therapy (Truax & Carkhuff, 1967).

9

Being *With* the Client

This chapter deals with the importance of the therapist's really being with the client: with her in content and in feeling. In terms of content, the good therapist conveys to her client a willingness and ability to follow the details of the client's story. *The therapist is seen by the client as someone who is continually trying to follow the client's story.* The therapist may get sidetracked sometimes. He or she may not recognize a name that the client mentions or a passing reference to an event that has been described before. When this happens, the therapist quickly admits it and asks the questions she needs answered to get on the track again. (I have described and given examples of these kinds of questions in the first part of Chapter 6, the section entitled "Preliminaries to Sharing—The Call for Feeling.") The therapist actively tries to follow what the client tells her. She does not give up trying to follow just because the client may seem to ramble. The client does not have to state every element clearly for her therapist to follow it; the therapist accepts unclear statements and works with the client toward clarifying their meaning. At times, the therapist may give brief summaries or short reflections of what she has understood the client to say. If her understanding is wrong, this gives the client an opportunity to perceive the therapist's errors and correct them. (The importance of being able to accept and adjust to the client's corrections, to honor her own expertness about her own story and feelings, is dealt with further in the next chapter.) When the therapist has successfully understood the story being told, these short summaries convey that understanding clearly to the client. Often the client herself has not focused clearly on the details of what she is saying. The therapist's summaries may help both of them to follow the main line of content together.

The therapist must, of course, be able to understand more than just the content of what the client says. She needs to have a sense of the feelings experienced by the client in the situations described. *The therapist is seen by the client as someone who tries to actively sense and enter into the feeling experiences of the client.* Carl Rogers has put the key aspect of this particularly clearly:

> To sense the client's private world as if it were your own, but without ever losing the "as if" quality—this is empathy, and this seems essential to therapy. To sense the client's anger, fear, or confusion as if it were your own, yet without your own anger, fear, or confusion getting bound up in it, is the condition we are endeavoring to describe. When the client's world is this clear to the therapist, and he moves about in it freely, then he can both communicate his understanding of what is clearly known to the client and can also voice meanings in the client's experience of which the client is scarcely aware (Rogers, 1961, p. 284).

This is the kind of sharing which I have tried to describe in the second part of Chapter 6, the section entitled "Sharing the Client's Experience." Here, as with understanding the content of the client's story, the therapist tries to share aloud what she thinks she senses of the client's experience. The involved, empathic therapist will convey this in active and frequently vividly phrased language. She does not let the client's feeling die away by repeating back the client's own words in a lackluster voice, nor does she freeze up the flow of feeling by rephrasing it into a technical or intellectualized jargon.

These two client perceptions—the therapist as someone who tries to follow the story and the therapist as someone who tries to share in the experienced feelings—are never really totally separate from each other. The factual content of what the client says in psychotherapy is rarely, if ever, devoid of important feelings, and the therapist responds to these at the same time that he or she responds to the content itself. Strong feelings may occur, at times, however, without their being obviously linked up to any particular content. Such feelings may be experienced and noted without their origin inmediately discerned. Most typically, though, content and feeling go together; and this mixture will be reflected in these excerpts from psychotherapy sessions.

Here is part of a therapy session between myself and a woman who was still living with her parents, but not very happy about it. Although we talked about feeling, it seems to me that the emphasis here is on following what she says rather than sharing in the experience of it. As always, of course, some of both happened.

C: I had to stay home all day yesterday, stayed downstairs, and it was terrible. I really felt anxious. It was just terrible.

T: Just a kind of nervous feeling all over?

C: Yes. That was it.

T: Can you tell me any more of what it felt like?

C: I kept thinking of the book *I Never Promised You a Rose Garden*, and I kept thinking of the voice shouting out at her. I didn't hear any voice, just kept thinking of it.

T: A voice shouting out what?

C: "You're not one of them."

T: Maybe you really didn't want to be one of them there.

C: No. I didn't.

T: Sort of saying, "Let that family be something different from me and me from it."

C: That's what I ask for all the time.

T: Kind of, a part of you is always saying to them "Won't you let me go?"

C: If only I didn't have to eat there.

T: Eating is an especially hard time?

C: I can't get out of it. That's the only thing.

T: You can't hide then.

She describes a situation, and I try by questioning to sense more about what it was like. I have read the novel she then mentions to me, an enormously moving story of an adolescent girl in a mental hsopital, but I do not recognize the particular part to which she has made reference and I feel free to ask her about it. She gives me the quote, and I try to show her that I understand its relationship to the situation she has been describing. I try to see both the picture she is drawing for me and to sense what it means to her.

With this next client, the emphasis is also primarily on following content rather than focusing on the feeling alone. She is talking about her relationship to her boyfriend. It is a relationship that has had a great number of ins and outs, and she has sometimes been too subtle in conveying to him when it was on the outs as far as she was concerned.

C: Our engagement . . . it was last January to this date, and it still has never been published. A ring, but it has been a completely informal engagement. And for the past month and a half now, I haven't worn the ring. I just didn't say anything and the stupid thing is he never . . . I mean never like saying, "Why aren't you wearing the ring?" Because he knew something was wrong, but not even being able to mention it.

T: Boy!

C: Not even to talk about it.

T: So you really tried to give him a hint. You didn't just wait around for him to ask about your feelings. You did more than that. Still nothing happened.

C: I . . . [lapses into silence].

T: You took the ring off. That's asking him to ask. It's making a first move, it's not just waiting. But it wasn't enough, it didn't help.

C: Right. I think . . . there are some very . . . I don't know, pondersome, difficult things on his mind which he can't face up to in himself.

I try to sense what she has done and why. I try to show her that I have been listening and trying to understand. My understanding seems to be right, and it enables her to move on to another area of their relationship, her boyfriend's difficulties in facing certain things in himself. This kind of movement is a frequent result of the client's sensing that the therapist has understood what happened. Gendlin (1964, 1968) has many interesting thoughts on this aspect of what he calls "focusing ability." When the client can (frequently with the help of her therapist) focus sharply and accurately on her own experience, she is then ready and able to move on to other experiences with which she could not deal before.

Sometimes the therapist can find words for a part of the client's story that might otherwise remain unspoken. The man in the following therapy excerpt is an undergraduate student, with eventual aspirations toward graduate school. He has been describing a psychology experiment in which he took part as a subject. He is talking now about the experimenter, a graduate student at the University.

C: He was . . . it was real interesting. Every time I think of that. He was doing it for his doctoral degree. All that seems so far away. That's wonderful though. He seems like a real nice guy, too. He's very young. I don't know, his looks are deceiving maybe, but he seemed like he was about 27.

T: It sounds as if you're saying maybe if you took part in an experiment for someone working on his doctorate that somehow the magic of the doctorate might rub off on you.

C: I knew right away I was attracted when he said "doctoral degree," because I said, this experiment is just for me. This guy is going for his doctorate. I'll be perfect for his experiment.

T: That's a status experiment.

C: Yes, I guess for me that's sure true.

My putting into words this aspect of what he was telling me helped draw our attention to this aspect of the client's motivation. His tone of voice made it clear, as the printed word here may not, that he accepted it and felt good about the recognition of it.

As the aspect of sharing a client's experienced feelings begins to dominate over simply understanding the contents, the emotional tone of the therapist's comments becomes heightened. The therapist conveys his or her emphatic experience of the client's world by the vividness and energy with which he engages in the dialogue. In this next therapy example, the client is struggling to make clear to me both what happened and how it felt. I try to reflect my understanding of both in my comments to him.

C: I was sitting in one of my classrooms, and there was this kid sitting next to me who I know a little, and he has a lot of bad qualities. He's a very shallow person and, you know, he's very false. And somehow I built up a fantasy in my mind of a relationship with me and him, and like . . . he said something or we were talking or something, and all of a sudden, I had a, a, a hate like I never felt before in my life! Something like . . . like all of a sudden I had the feeling in my stomach and I felt so scared. Honestly, in class I just went like this [*makes a gesture of clenching his muscles in extreme tension, and then relaxing them suddenly as if in despair and surprise that nothing has happened*], because, like, I couldn't handle it anymore, and then I sat down and then I calmed down a little.

T: You started, like, making up a story.

C: Yeah!

T: You daydreamed the story to yourself, and then the dialogue got so hot, you got madder and madder, that, Jesus! You just wanted to kill

Being With *the Client* 81

the bastard. And nothing had happened, he was still just sitting there in front of you!

C: Right! Exactly that!

The heightened feeling of my comments seemed to act partly to give him permission to feel strongly. If I can respond with strong feelings, then strong feelings may not always be wrong. This excerpt also reflects the importance of responding to visual as well as vocal communication.

Just as focusing on content may help a client move on to a new area, an accurate and vivid reflection of his or her feelings may help him or her move from one feeling to another. The therapy passage I've chosen to illustrate this would be much clearer if you could hear it as well as read it. The printed word can, however, give some notion of what took place.

C: I was walking over to work today and I saw this girl who I met at camp when I worked there. And she said, "I've been so depressed about . . ." she wanted to get engaged, and the boyfriend doesn't want to. She's a student, he's teaching, and she keeps saying, you know, "Let's get engaged so that we can set a date to get married and everything." She was so worried. And I said to her, "Don't worry about it. Just take it as it comes." But I can't look at it that way. I can't relate to that myself. Because today doesn't represent anything. I told her that today doesn't . . .

T: Maybe there is an answer, but it's one that is no good for you, because things aren't real enough for you right now. There is kind of an emptiness in everything.

C: So I gave in before I went to work, and I had a tuna fish sandwich and a container of milk. And I was so hungry that I just chewed the tuna fish sandwich, I mean just taking bite by bite and chewing it. It tasted so good. [*His tone of voice does not yet sound "good" but it has taken on a slightly different note than the despairing sound it has had so far.*]

T: Why is that a giving in? I don't understand.

C: Well, this way, I won't be able to run the car, 'cause I'm short of money and it will run out of gas. And I just . . . [*his voice takes on a firmness of sound*] I just tasted the tuna fish and just relished it, it was so good.

T: It was real.

C: Yes, it was so real!

T: An honest to God tuna fish sandwich there. Out of all that nothing. Tasted like tuna fish, and you couldn't mistake it. That's good.

C: And I love tuna fish, so that's the greatest thing in the world.

It seems to me that because I could accurately sense his emptiness and despair, he could trust me not to lose sight of it and thus share a more positive feeling with me, as well. And because I was able to catch quickly, too, his capacity for that positive feeling, he was able to share aloud for both of us his ability to find joy in a tuna fish sandwich.

As I noted before, sometimes feelings are there to be recognized even when content and motives are unclear. The feelings are no less real for that. Here is another excerpt from therapy with the man quoted above.

C: I just started to cry. And I don't know why. There is just no reason for it.

T: You couldn't really say why you were crying, except that it hurts so much you're crying.

C: Yeah, you know, like I told you last time, there is nothing, there is nothing I can pinpoint. You know, it's not sex, or it's not like trouble getting along, it's like everything should be O.K. I don't know, it's . . . I can't find any answer.

T: Then something isn't O.K. Something in there really hurts.

C: I can't find . . . it just . . . there is no apparent answer, there is no reason for it, it just shouldn't be there.

T: It shouldn't be there?

C: Well, there's no need for it.

T: But the reaction I get is that you're giving yourself more of a lecture now about how to shape up. Kind of like, "Look here now, pull yourself together, nothing is wrong." Boy! You know better than that! You sound like what somebody would say to you who didn't really know that you really hurt.

C: Well, I just guess that's the only way I know how to react.

This client is beginning to see how he reacts to himself like an admonishing parent. I'm implicitly sharing with him a value which is important to me: The idea that what *is* comes before what *should* be. He will eventually make his own value judgments about himself, but I want those judgments to be based on an honest recognition of what his experiences are. What I had to share here was valued by him because he trusted me to be real. The therapist who is open to his own experiences and who can share in those of the client helps the client to become a more congruent person, a person who can know what he truly feels.

Some Relevent Research

The research I shall sample here deals with the concept of empathy. It is, then, most relevant to my fourth client perception: *that the therapist is seen by the client as someone who tries to actively sense and enter into the feeling experiences of the client.* There seems to be no research dealing with the preceding client perception—the importance of the therapist being seen as someone who understands the factual details, story line, and content of what the client is seeing. Perhaps that element is simply taken for granted. Perhaps it is assumed to be important, with writers also assuming that all therapists do it. The first of those assumptions may be correct; my experience, and the experiences of clients I have talked with, leads me to believe the second assumption is not. In any case, formal research has no contribution to make here.

The Barrett-Lennard (1962) study referred to in the preceding chapter is well worth noting again. The Relationship Inventory used in that study has, as noted previously, a scale designed to measure empathic understanding. As with the other scales, the client rated each statement for how true or untrue it was of her therapist. A few examples of statements that produce empathy scores are: "He tries to see things through my eyes." "He is interested in knowing what my experiences mean to me." "When I do not say what I mean at all clearly, he still understands me." Barrett-Lennard found that improvement in psychotherapy was significantly related to how high an empathic understanding score the therapist received from her client.

Barrett-Lennard also had one form of Relationship Inventory filled out by the psychotherapists. For example, the item "he tries to see things through my eyes" becomes in the therapist form: "I try to see things through his eyes." Some of the therapists in that research study were very experienced, while others had limited experience in psychotherapy. Barrett-Lennard found that the experienced therapists were much more likely to agree with their clients' ratings of how much empathy they offered than were the inexperienced therapists. To know whether or not a client regards the therapist as empathic requires a good level of empathy. To the extent that more experienced therapists may be better therapists, their accuracy in knowing the degree of empathy their clients experience with them is further support for the importance of empathy in good psychotherapy. Rogers and his coworkers (1967), working with hospitalized schizophrenic clients, also studied the relationship between the level of empathy, regard, and congruence which therapists felt they were offering, and the levels of these qualities which clients saw themselves as receiving. In general, therapists and clients agreed very little; but the therapist's understanding of what his client perceived in him tended to be related to improvement in therapy.

Truax defined his concept of "accurate empathy" as involving "both the therapist's sensitivity to current feelings and his verbal facility to communicate this understanding in a language attuned to the client's current feelings" (Truax & Carkhuff, 1967, p. 46). This definition is well in line with the concept offered here; empathy is not enough, it must be communicated in a way that the client can perceive. Truax's scale for the measurement of accurate empathy is given in the book with Carkhuff (Truax & Carkhuff, 1967) from which this definition is drawn. A number of studies involving the scale are summarized there. Perhaps future research will clarify the question of whether or not Truax's "accurate empathy" scale measures that quality which his verbal definition of accurate empathy presents. In any case, it appears to measure some important concept, related to empathy and/or therapist congruence, which is significantly correlated with success in psychotherapy. A study comparing psychoanalytic therapy with behavior therapy (Sloan, et al., 1975) did not find a clear relationship between therapy outcome and outside observers' ratings of "accurate empathy." Both kinds of therapy did, however, yield clear connections between successful outcome and the clients' own judgments of how much empathy they experienced.

I have suggested that the *attempt* to understand and experience a client's feelings is the key factor, provided the attempt is sometimes successful. There is some research support for this. Rogers (1961) cites an unpublished doctoral dissertation by Quinn (1950) which apparently produced a similar finding. Rogers' judgment is that "it shows that 'understanding' of the client's meanings is essentially an attitude of desiring to understand." He finds it "rather conclusive evidence that it is an attitude of wanting to understand which is communicated" (Rogers, 1961, p. 44).

10

Respect for the Client

This chapter deals with the two final client perceptions listed in Chapter 5. Both have to do with respect for the client. The first is: *The therapist is seen by the client as someone who considers the client worthy of being helped.* It is the client's sense that his or her fate matters to the therapist. He does not feel that he is seen only as an object to be serviced, but as a human being to be helped. He knows that he is seen as a client, but he also knows that this is not a debased role. It is, rather, a valued one. The therapist is there to help him because he is of value and worthy of being helped. The therapist is regarded as both respectful and caring, and as someone who is friendly and warm toward the client—not as someone who does not care what happens. The therapist is not just curious about the way the client functions, but is really interested in him as a person. This kind of interaction with the therapist can be a source of new self-esteem for the client (just as interactions in which the client holds a debased role can be a source of new self-rejection).

This kind of acceptance of the client is closely related to another kind of respectful attitude. *The therapist is seen by the client as someone who respects the client's right to be the final judge of his or her own feelings and experiences.* As noted in earlier sections of this book, the therapist tries to share in the foremost feeling experiences which the client has at a given moment. He tries to put into vivid language and voice the feelings he thinks the client may be experiencing. His suggested formulations are just that—"suggestions." If they ring true to the client, they will be useful and lead to something new. If they do not ring true, both the client and therapist try to reach an understanding of the situation. Only the client can be the judge of the correctness of these "suggestions" or "interpretations." The fact that the therapist's statements may be an accurate representation of some aspect of the client's world which is not yet strongly felt, or on which the client has not yet focused, is both trivial and useless. It is not part of a therapist's role in the therapy hour to be correct about the overall history or dynamics of some semi-abstract case history. He is concerned with what the client is saying and feeling then, at that moment, and must respect the client's reactions to his interpretations.

The therapist appreciates what the client's experiences mean to the client. His understanding of the client depends to a large extent on how the client feels about himself. The therapist is not perceived as someone who thinks that only he is capable of correctly interpreting feelings and experiences. He does not argue with the client when there is disagreement, and does not try to convince the client that his interpretations are correct. The therapist does not force the client to accept the therapist's point of view.

The reader may ask here: "But what if the client unconsciously or even consciously deceives the therapist about the feelings involved; what if he denies the therapist's description of the feelings when the therapist is really right?" That is one possible error. My experience has been that it is a self-correcting error. When a reasonably congruent, respectful therapist misses an important feeling of the client's (for whatever reason) the client will express the feeling to him again. Another error—the therapist's insistence on the correctness of his interpretation despite the client's honest disagreement—is far more serious. The bond of trust and mutual respect is weakened, and there may not be a second chance to correct it. A client may, of course, seek psychotherapy because he is confused about feelings. But it seems that the therapist who is most likely to be able to help him clarify his feelings is one who also respects his integrity and developing self-knowledge.

Sometimes in the course of psychotherapy, the client himself questions the reality and importance of his own feelings. He does not seem to view himself as worth being helped or as being an expert in his own feeling experiences. At such times, it may take the caring and respect of the therapist to allow the client to be in touch with and to express his own real feelings. The client in the psychotherapy session quoted from below had telephoned me the previous night. He had seemed desperately lonely and afraid. Now he is questioning his own feelings.

C: Like it's all phony. Like I'm making it all up. I'm giving myself an excuse for something. No. I don't know that, I don't even understand that. I don't think it is . . . I don't know what it is.

T: You're just afraid that you're some sort of kid that is overdramatizing his upset, making a big deal out of it.

C: Yes, and I'm afraid of what people think. Like I didn't know whether you thought that . . . last night on the phone.

T: I can answer that. I don't think it's phony, Phil. I think your hurt is real.

C: [*Suddenly beginning to cry*] I could die. I can't stop. I don't understand it. I can't stop. I have no reason, I just . . . I can't think of anything to do or any way to act, I don't know.

T: Just so lost. Just reaching out every place, and just no way to know.

C: And I can't seem to . . . like this, I can't, I just, there's no reason for it.

T: You think to yourself, you think to yourself, "My God, it's just so bad." You don't want to think of more days like this.

C: And she [*his girfriend*] is the only thing that keeps me going, because if I didn't love her, if I didn't care . . . that's the only thing that's real, the only thing I could hold on to.

T: You've got to love someone else just to keep yourself alive.

C: I hate it. I hate it so much. [*His voice has moved through the despairing sadness of his crying to the anger of the last few words. Now he speaks in a calmer tone—as if having experienced a sense of relief.*] Do you have a tissue?

T: I'm all out of them. I'm badly equipped. No, I don't, [*offering his handkerchief*] even that's not very clean. I'm sorry.

C: I'm O.K.

T: Medium good shape.

He was worthy of being heard and being helped when he phoned me the night before. I respected his doubts about his own feelings, and his worries about his phoniness, and I tried to share with him my respect for those doubts and fears. But I also trusted the feelings that he had spoken of, even when he doubted them. I shared that trust and the caring that goes with it, and that seemed to make it easier for him to understand those feelings, to find some expression for them and to move on.

This kind of respect also means a sharing of responsibility. I try to help my client and always assume that he is a partner in these efforts. Some aspects of him, some ways of reacting, may be working against our joint goal, but I know that a part of him always works with me, too. Neither do I ever allow him to do the work entirely alone, as long as we are seeing each other in therapy. I am there to help. A brief excerpt below from a therapy session between myself and another man may help illustrate this interplay.

C: But I can't help thinking that something else in me is pushing, really, really pushing me, because I don't always believe the things I seem to do. Something in me makes me just organize those papers over and over again. I don't believe that organizing would make any difference. I don't believe it, but there is a force in there that pushes me and that can't be the same person that says you don't have to do it. I am trapped in my own mind, but it's not like my mind, it's like somebody else's.

T: Right, something like you were saying before. There does seem to be some part of you, in you, that is causing this mess. But another thing you're saying, Brian, is that there is a part of you that's not. There's a part of you that has the experience of being able to look at things and makes sense out of them. So your mind is not only the silly part or the stupid part of whatever it is you want to call it.

C: I guess it's just something I have to think about.

T: It's something we have to think about more together, too.

I believe his feelings of confusion, and indicate that I hear them. I believe that something pushes him into senseless acts, and I let him know. But I also hear, trust, and respect the part of him that is not senseless, and I speak of that to him, too. When he promises to give this more thought, he is assured that he does not have to do it alone. He has come for help, he is worthy of it, and I offer the best I can.

I noted in Chapter 7, in the beginning stages of psychotherapy, that I try to teach my clients to feel free to disagree with me. I want them to tell me when my statements about what they seem to be feeling ring false to them. This is very much a part of what I mean by respecting the client's right to be the final judge of his own feelings and experiences. Such a reminder is given in a therapy excerpt below, part of the same session which has just been quoted. It is considerably earlier in the session, and the client is discussing his college roommate.

C: He could be so much better a person, you know, better for himself, if he would just put the notes in order and just study them. He doesn't even have to study his math notes if he doesn't want to but it would be so nice. Just so he would have them. Just so the work he does doesn't seem like it's lost. To me it seems like a loss, he spends so much time taking those notes, and then doesn't even keep them in order.

T: It must also seem that when you spend so much time on certain things, when you work so hard at keeping things in order, then when somebody could be sloppy and get away with it, it's almost like a reproach to you.

C: Right.

T: Here is somebody who can make nothing of things that are tough for you, who doesn't have to bother with them at all.

C: That's true. [hesitantly] It's really true. I never thought of that before.

T: Well, like my other suggestions, you've got to test it out against your feelings. It may be wrong.

C: Right. But, he's really happy even though he doesn't care. He doesn't have to worry about grades really. He's just so happy in being so utterly disorganized, and I have to be . . . you know, just having the papers is not enough for me. They have to be in an order that has no order, and they have to be exact. It's so stupid.

Perhaps it was his tone of voice which suggested that this compulsively orderly student experienced his roommate's casual manner as a reproach. The response, "That's true . . . I never thought of that before," appears to be a way of saying "I have felt just that, but I have never put it into words." I reminded him, as I had before, that he is the final judge of his feelings and experiences. He must guard against my errors. After all (and I have spoken to him about this before), if I had to wait to speak until I was absolutely certain, I might end up saying nothing at all.

Sometimes I interpret the feeling just right, sometimes not. There have already been examples in this book of suggestions or hunches of mine which clients rejected. Here is another example.

C: Like, sometimes I sit in a room, and I want people to come in, and say hello to me. This is why I goof a lot about not getting mail or phone calls or anything like that. It's not really so funny. In fact it isn't funny at all. [*The sound of fearfulness is in her voice.*]

T: And you're all alone, and sort of scared of being even more alone.

C: No. I'm not so afraid of being alone. It isn't that. I got over that fear last summer. The only thing I'm afraid of is that when I'm alone now, I get to the point where I don't want to be with anybody because I'm really digging this bit of being alone.

T: Let me see if I'm hearing it right. It isn't that you're scared of being alone, but that something is happening to you so that the aloneness doesn't matter. You don't want to change that way.

C: You see what happens. I've gone from one extreme to the other. I'm afraid of not caring.

I heard her fear but mistook the nature of it. It is not being alone that frightens her now; she no longer wants or cares about other people that much. The fear is that she will continue to be a person who cares less and less about others. She corrected me, and I tried again. This time I came close enough so that we could move on.

I want to emphasize that my opinion that the client is the final judge of his own feelings and experiences is not limited to relatively healthy clients. I also listen closely to what hospitalized mental clients tell me of their feelings and of how close I have come to understanding them. I am the expert in thinking of possibilities and finding words to express them. They are the experts in deciding which possibilities fit.

Some Relevant Research

There is some fairly clear evidence that even deeply disturbed individuals are sensitive to the feelings that occur in psychotherapy. In a study of psychotherapy with hospitalized persons diagnosed as schizophrenic, Rogers (1967) had both the clients and their therapists fill out the Barrett-Lennard Relationship Inventory. The amount of congruence, acceptance, and empathy which the clients felt they were receiving from their therapists was often quite different from the amount the therapists themselves thought they were offering. Tape recordings of those therapy sessions were then played for a group of college students who were neither therapists nor clients. These outside observers also filled out the Relationship Inventory, and they clearly agreed much more closely with the ratings given by the schizophrenics than with the ratings given by the therapists.

In the Barrett-Lennard (1962) study, which was discussed in the research sections of the last two chapters, some relationship was found between the level of regard (the typical amount of caring and respect given to the client) and the client's improvement in therapy. The finding was not as marked, however, as was that between improvement and the congruence of the therapist. There was also a suggestion that congruence (therapist openness and honesty) and "unconditionality of regard" might sometimes be at odds with each other. The study by Mills and Zytowski (1967), also discussed previously in this book, adds further weight to that last finding. They found that when the level of regard for the client is too high, too constant, empathy may become somewhat inaccurate and congruence disturbed. Perhaps the appropriate consideration here is that the client should be considered worthy and valuable, but not superhuman. It is also clear from their findings that level of regard is more important than unconditionality of regard (liking him an equal amount all the time). It is difficult to really care about someone and never vary the level of caring. As they put it: "In other words, the more one person accepts all behaviors of the other person in a relationship, the lower the level of his characteristic response to that person" (Mills & Zytowski, 1967, p. 196).

Truax talks about a construct he calls "nonpossessive warmth," which seems to have many of the characteristics of the qualities described in this chapter. In a book summarizing much of his research (Truax & Carkhuff, 1967), he presents data which strongly suggest that nonpossessive warmth is, indeed, another important contribution to favorable outcome in psychotherapy.

Finally, three research studies discussed in Chapter 3 are relevant here (Board, 1959; Feifel & Eells, 1963; Strupp, Wallach & Wogan, 1964). Each of these explored the client's view of the therapy relationship and the client's view of the outcome of his psychotherapy. The feeling that the therapist offered liking and respect was strongly related to the feeling that therapy had been of help.

11

Concluding Therapy

I do not think there is any natural total conclusion to psychotherapy. If it has been a good relationship, then it could probably continue to be a relationship in which further growth could take place no matter how much has already happened. In practice, however, there comes a time when the client and psychotherapist stop meeting together for their regular sessions. This may come about in a number of ways. Both parties may agree that it is time to terminate their sessions. Outside circumstances may dictate a conclusion to psychotherapy. The client may wish to terminate therapy, although the therapist may not feel that it is a good time to do so. The therapist may decide that therapy sessions should come to an end, although the client may disagree; or finally, a time limit may have been set at the beginning of the therapy.

Both Client and Therapist Agree to Terminate

Holland (1965) has given a nice description of a situation that often occurs near the end of helpful psychotherapy. "Just as the psychotherapist is beginning to wonder how much more he needs to do or ought to do with the patient, the latter begins to indicate in subtle ways that he is beginning to consider the same questions" (p. 270). In other words, client and therapist sense at about the same time that therapy is coming to an end. It has been a helpful and growing experience for the client and to some extent for the therapist also. The client senses now that it is time for him or her to devote this energy to other relationships, to the more natural relationships one finds in life, and to do more growing through those. She feels more ready to do that now than when she first came for therapy. Whatever sources of personal discomfort led her to seek help have now vanished or at least greatly diminished. The therapist, too, senses that this has happened. He still enjoys his sessions with the client, he still feels he can be of some help, but he knows too that the client is ready to do her growing elsewhere. The therapist is also aware that other individuals need therapeutic help more than this client currently does, and perhaps he should make the hours available for them.

Perhaps the therapist is the first to mention this view; perhaps the client is. Whoever says it first quickly finds an answering chord in the other. Perhaps they decide to try spacing out sessions, making them less frequent. Most often, though, this kind of jointly agreed ending to psychotherapy seems to come to a natural full stop within two or three sessions after the topic of termination has been raised. Talk of termination is often important from the very beginning of therapy. But a short time after it is raised in serious and practical terms and recognized by both parties, the psychotherapy sessions are over. It is probably this kind of ending to psychotherapy that Steinzor forecasts for his client in his fine book on psychotherapy, *The Healing Partnership* (1967). He says " 'when a patient asks how long will therapy take?' I can answer, 'For the rest of your life—and I wish you a very long one.' And I add, 'But our meetings will cease as quickly as we can possibly help you become involved in relations which aren't dull and in which you can act spontaneously' " (p. 13).

In my terms, our sessions end when the client is ready to make good and active use of the nontherapy parts of his or her life as a growing experience. I reserve the term "therapy" for our sessions together, but I never fool myself for a moment into thinking that this is the only kind of situation in which an individual learns and grows. When a client and I come to this view of the situation at about the same time, therapy ends as I have described it here.

Termination Due to Outside Circumstances

I wonder how much of all the psychotherapy that is done is done by experienced psychotherapists. A great deal of it is certainly done by therapists in training. The therapist in training is typically assigned only temporarily to a clinic or hospital. Most of his or her clients have to terminate therapy with her when her training needs and demands take her elsewhere. This is the most common outside circumstance that brings an end to psychotherapy.

I think it is essential that a therapist who is only temporarily assigned to a clinic should tell his or her client at the beginning of therapy that there is an outside limit on the time they can spend together. Obviously, this is essential in order to maintain what I see as the essential truthfulness of psychotherapy. In addition, knowing there is a time limit on their therapy, therapist and client can focus their activities and goals in a different way. At the end of this chapter, I shall present some material about purposely setting time limits in psychotherapy for the helpfulness of the limits themselves. Time limits set by outside circumstances can also be helpful. I have found in doing psychotherapy in a university clinic that regardless of when a client has begun therapy, he or she tends to show marked progress near the end of the school year. Because of the accelerating and pace-setting nature of outside limits, I tend to play down one of the options that is also open: It is usually possible in clinic settings for a client to be seen further by another therapist. If you are working in an internship type of setting which you must leave at the end of the year, I suggest putting it to your client this way: "Let's consider your psychotherapy limited by the time you and I have together. If things do go wrong after I leave, you can phone here and I'll leave word for them to try to find another therapist for you. That will probably work out if you want it to, but I'd like you to try first to see what happens without that. See how things go for you for a while without psychotherapy. Then if you feel it's important—and you are the judge of this—you phone them up here, and I'm almost certain that they will be able to arrange for someone to see you."

Sometimes the outside circumstances are dictated by the events of the client's life. Clients finish school, change jobs, move to different parts of the country. I think that these events, when the client and therapist know of them somewhat in advance, always have at least some helpful and pace-setting quality. That quality can be destroyed by a therapist who reacts anxiously or pessimistically to the circumstances, but I think that the potential of their being somewhat helpful, as well as inevitably limiting, is always there.

The Client Wishes to Terminate before the Therapist Does

The finely timed agreement about termination described at the beginning of this chapter does not always take place. Sometimes the client will announce that she feels ready to end psychotherapy before the therapist has thought about doing so. In the abstract, I can imagine situations in which the therapist might forcibly argue with the client about the importance of her staying on. For example, if the therapist feels that the client is an active physical danger to herself or to others, it might seem to the therapist an ethical imperative to urge the client to renain in therapy. In practice, however, I have never tried to talk a client out of ending therapy with me. I may not give her my full agreement. I may suggest she come for another two or three sessions so that we can think things over together, or I may suggest that we try having sessions two or three weeks apart for a while to see how things progress. If the client rejects these alternatives, though, then I honor without argument her judgment that our therapy has come to an end. Naturally, I try to understand the reasons for our termination, just as I try to understand her feelings about other issues. I do not try to understand mainly for my sake, but because I am still in a therapeutic interaction with her until the time when we no longer see each other again.

One of the good results of not arguing with clients who wish to terminate therapy is that the therapist is able to leave the door open to clients in such a way that they can call again without losing face. I never suggest in any way that clients are wrong to stop therapy with me. I never say, "You wait and see how sorry you are, and then you'll call me, and I'm so nice I'll see you again then." I tell them something more like, "If that's what seems best to you, then I think that's what you should do. I share my hunches with you, but you're the expert on yourself. I think we have made some real progress here. It sounds like it's time for you to take that progress and concentrate on using it in your other relationships. Of course, if for any reason you ever want to call me, please feel free." As far as I can judge from experience with my clients, they seem able to use this message. I have had clients phone me again a number of times, and it seems they have always accepted it as a fairly natural thing rather than as a new source of failure.

Up to this point, we have considered cases where the client feels he or she made at least some significant progress during psychotherapy. But a client sometimes decides to terminate therapy because she feels she has made little or no progress, even though the therapist may feel that some significant gains are being made. The client has to be the final judge of what is happening to her. As always, the therapist can and should present the situation as he or she sees it—here are the things the therapist thinks have happened in psychotherapy; here, if the therapist feels it is appropriate to the client's needs to share them, are the therapist's feelings about the client's wish to terminate. Perhaps the therapist suggests another session or two to think things through. But, as before, the client is helped to leave, and left free to call again, without any strong argument or loss of face. If the client still wants to seek some sort of psychotherapy, the therapist should be willing to suggest names of other therapists who might possibly better meet the needs of this client.

The Therapist Wishes to Terminate before the Client Does

Because I believe the client is the expert on herself, I proceed more slowly when I believe that the client is ready to terminate therapy and she disagrees. Yet sometimes I insist upon having my way. If I feel strongly enough that the client is ready and able to seek her growing experiences elsewhere (and I know there are other less able persons waiting for my free hours), I urge us to soon bring therapy to an end. I do not stop immediately. In this situation, I am likely to suggest that we taper off gradually—perhaps meet every other week for a while instead of once a week. There is a potential danger in this sort of process. Theoretically at least, if the client wants badly enough to stay with me, she may produce new and more severe symptoms as her bid for the right to remain. However, I simply have never had this happen. Perhaps it has not happened because my judgment has been fairly good about the client being growth-oriented at the time termination was suggested—the client preferred expanding experiences to new symptoms. Another thing that may help ward off such unfortunate circumstances is, again, leaving the door open. I seriously tell my client that I want her to try doing without therapy, and I trust that she will comply. Because of this trust, I am free to tell her she may call me again. These calls rarely come.

A somewhat similar situation occurred with a college student whom I had seen in therapy the previous year. We both felt that therapy had come to a successful conclusion, although he was somewhat more doubtful about this than I. Shortly after the end of the summer vacation, he came to see me again. He asked if he could come in just once in a while. "Perhaps every other week or even once in three weeks" just to talk a little. I promised to accept him on this basis, and we set a future appointment before I had given it much thought. As I gave it more thought, I became concerned. I urged him to tell me more about why he still wanted to see me. "I like you and I find you easy to talk to," he told me. "You know, it's hard to make new friends and get really close to people, and if I know you are going to be here I can look forward to coming in and being with you." I told him that I thought this was a "cop out." I told him, honestly, that I was pleased that he liked me and wanted to talk with me, but that I felt he should be forming new close relationships elsewhere. I was afraid that coming in to see me was too easy, and therefore he might not do the sometimes hard work of making new friends. Would he please think this over, I requested, and let me know soon how he felt about it. He telephoned me before the scheduled time of our next appointment to say that he had thought it over and agreed. I think he trusted my promise that I would see him again if he did not agree with me; I'm glad he agreed.

Preset Time Limits

Some therapists have experimented with setting time limits at the beginning of therapy. There is an interesting experimental study on these active time limits by Shlien, Mosak, and Dreikurs (1962). Two different theoretical orientations to psychotherapy were involved, the client-centered therapy of Carl Rogers and Adlerian therapy. Half of the client-centered clients were given no time limits on their therapy, while the other half were told that they could have a maximum of twenty sessions of therapy; the same split was done for the Adlerian clients. The technique used to measure their progress and improvement in psychotherapy was a measure that determines the distance between one's view of one's self and one's view of one's *ideal* self. The study also involved a group of persons seeking psychotherapy but not yet receiving it. For these potential clients, there was on the average no change over time in the difference between the self and the ideal self. A group of nonclients was also studied; their picture of self and ideal self was much closer together than that of the clients, but it also showed no change in the average over time. All four groups of clients in therapy showed changes in the same direction—the difference between self and ideal self became less. In other words, they became, in a sense, more accepting of themselves. To judge from previous studies using this technique (the authors of this one do not give details), both "self" and "ideal" changed. They became more like what they wished to be, and their ideal goal became less rigid. Those clients who were given unlimited therapy had an average of 37 interviews, while the time-limited clients actually terminated after an average of eighteen interviews. Both at the time of termination and after a year's follow-up, there were no measurable differences between the time-limited and the unlimited clients. In other words, the time-limited therapy was as effective as the unlimited therapy and it was twice as *efficient*.

The clients in this thought-provoking study were all clinic outpatients. I do not know how widely these findings can be generalized. Clearly, for many clients, time can certainly be saved by setting a limit at the beginning of therapy. I find this, though, a difficult thing to do. Since I know there is some chance the client may need me longer, I cannot bring myself to say at the very beginning of therapy, "You may have a maximum of twenty hours of my time, and no more." Needless to say, the time limit, once set, cannot be casually changed without trust in the therapist and probably in therapy becoming severely impaired.

Freud suggested that time limits were sometimes useful during psychoanalysis. When he used them, he set them sometime during the analysis rather than at the very beginning. He warned, however, that such limits might be a hindrance and harmful at times. Unfortunately, he seemed to have no specific suggestion as to how to determine when they could be helpfully used; he felt it was up to the sensitivity of the analyst. "Nor can any general rule be laid down as to the right time for resorting to this forcible technical method: the analyst must use his own tact in the matter" (Freud, 1950, p. 319).

If a client seems to need treatment and still desires it after the time limits are up, it is theoretically possible to transfer him or her to another therapist. I wonder, though, if this isn't a partial betrayal of the limits which were announced at the beginning. I am not sure. The issue of time limits is a perplexing one; it seems to me that more thinking and more active research must be done.

12

Emergencies

This chapter deals with some of the emergency situations with which a psychotherapist must deal. The first section is about suicide threats and dangers. Next, some notes are given on dealing with those extreme breaks with reality which are often called "psychotic breaks." Following these, there is a section on the special problems which the need for hospitalization and drug therapy raises for the nonphysician psychotherapist. Finally, there are several examples of emergencies that came via phone calls and how I dealt with them. The chapter is a *sampling* of emergency problems; it is not, and probably could not be, a coverage of all the emergencies that may face a psychotherapist.

Suicide Threats and Dangers

In my opinion, there is no issue in therapy which touches more acutely on the specific and individual values of each psychotherapist than the danger of suicide. It raises questions for which some of us have answers—perhaps only tentative ones—but for which there is no common answer that offers comfort to all of us. Is suicide always wrong? Is suicide always a sign of severe mental disturbance? Are there conditions extreme enough to justify suicide? Should there be rules about suicide established by society? Must suicide always be a totally individual decision and respected as such? More questions and more forms of these questions might be added, but the list is long enough.

I find two apparent paradoxes in my own thoughts and actions. Seated alone at my desk, I find it impossible to come to a satisfactory answer to such questions. On the other hand, in interaction with a client I have never sat silent in the face of a serious suicide threat, nor have I merely shared my confusion; I have found that I had something to say. The second paradox rests on the one thought which most nearly comes clear when I am alone at my desk: It seems to me that a person should have the right to take his or her own life. But almost every time a client has seemed to be seriously and actively considering ending her life, I have talked with her in a way designed to prevent suicide. I have tried to let the final decision be her own, but I have also tried to bring to that decision facts and considerations which would turn it in the direction of continuing to live. (Of course some situations, such as intense and intractable physical pain, usually do not come before the psychotherapist; these will not be discussed here.)

I find in myself a faith that the human beings who come to see me have the potential to continue to change and grow in ways which they will experience as good. I cannot guarantee to help everyone who comes to me, but I have the conviction that some amount of positive growth is possible. I do my best to help it occur. As the client re-examines her life and ways of living, she may make one kind of change, then another, back and forth, in her struggle to find the way that she experiences as forward. But suicide is a different kind of decision, a different kind of change; it is an end of changing. I am personally in favor of continual change, not changelessness. I have a strong general preference in favor of life over death. Moreover, I am against irreversible decisions.

I can and do share these value positions of mine with my clients. They are my value judgments, and clients must examine them for what they are worth to them. With all my intellectual doubts and a great desire to be fair about the situation, I still seem to favor a strong recommendation against suicide.

I always take talk of suicide seriously. Sometimes such talk turns out to be a way of expressing a set of feelings, rather than a real plan for action. It is those feelings which are of importance then. I cannot think of any reason for dismissing a patient's talk of suicide lightly or with casual or sarcastic disbelief. The intensity and seriousness of the therapist's concern may show in different ways. The form it takes at a particular moment is determined by what is happening to the client and by the therapist's planned and also intuitive responses. Several years ago, I was seeing in therapy a man who had already seen quite a few therapists. He had given each of them up after a shorter or longer try. We had had about half a dozen sessions together. That evening he had announced almost casually that he had bought a gun. He was planning to use it if he found he was becoming psychotic again (something he knew and dreaded from his part). He told me that if he saw himself moving in that path he would put the barrel of the pistol in his mouth and fire. "For God's sake!" I found myself exclaiming, "Don't do it that way. I've seen guys on neurology wards who have blown half their heads off that way, who didn't die, who ended up living like some sort of miserable animal." The slight edge of flippancy with which he had announced his intention now vanished completely. I had not met his opening comment with a dispassionate "Tell me more about it." I had not drawn on my knowledge of his homosexual concerns to make a possibly correct, but certainly useless, interpretation of the symbolic meaning of putting a gun barrel in his mouth. I had met him immediately with belief and concern. It is my best guess that this belief and concern (which might, of course, have taken other forms as well) were important factors in our acceptance of each other and led to his remaining in therapy with me.

When we discuss someone's possible intention to take his own life, we frequently use the term "suicide threat." It seems to me that this usage reflects our feeling that suicide is not only a weapon against the self, but is also a threat and weapon against others. Samuel Weiss (1969) has written an interesting article which stresses this vindictive aspect of suicide. He acknowledges that vindictiveness is not the only motive for suicide, but he feels that it is the main one in the clients we see. Frequently the revenge motive is directed against family members who will supposedly feel sorry or guilty after the client's death. Weiss stresses to his clients that people do manage to get over or repress these guilt feelings rather quickly, making such a strategy useless. He also warns them that suicide attempts frequently fail and "lead to a state of paralysis which would then preclude another suicide attempt . . .

there is always the chance of becoming maimed and afflicted with more pain." This is, clearly, very much in line with what I told the client described above. Weiss also reports using religious arguments of different types: a strategy that I am not personally comfortable with. Sometimes, however, I point out to nonreligious clients the futility of thinking that they can enjoy their vindictiveness or revenge. The fantasy that the successful suicide will somehow be able to "watch" the results of his or her action is an important part of the vindictive motive for suicide. There seem to me to be both religious and nonreligious arguments suggesting that this will not be possible. If you want to influence the living, and particularly if you want to see your influence on the living, you must stay among them.

Another major and frequent motivation for suicide is loneliness: the desperate loneliness of feeling that no one cares whether you live or die. In one sense, loneliness is a kind of pain, and to turn from that pain in an attempt to take one's own life is similar to fleeing from intense physical pain. But I think loneliness is also frequently the intensifying factor which adds to the other motives for suicide. It is as if the potential suicide says to himself: "If someone cared about me, I could bear the hate I feel from others. If someone cared about my pain, that caring would help me to tolerate that pain. If there were closeness and companionship in living, I would have something to prefer to the utter loneliness with which one meets his own death."

I care whether my client lives or dies. I let him or her know that. There is, of course, a risk in making this clear to him. If he is motivated by feelings of revenge, against me as well as others, he may attempt suicide more readily because my caring provides a possibility of hurting me. Weiss (1969), in the article noted above, put his answer to the problem in this way: "It is emphasized to the client that the therapist would be sorry for the loss of a human, but the therapist would still have to be at work in his office at this regular schedule" (p. 40). I make my caring stronger than this; I make it clear that I am concerned with this special human being and that his loss would pain me. But I make it clear, too, that I will survive that loss. In a way, this follows from my feeling that therapy is directed primarily toward the needs of the client and not of the therapist. I wish my client well and feel a sense of pain at things which bring him ill, but I do not need him.

I shall return to some of these themes later in this chapter when discussing how to handle emergency phone calls. One more point needs to be made about the suicide dangers that come to the surface during the therapy hour. This point is the recognition that the suicide threat or thought may not be spoken easily aloud. Obviously, if a suicide thought is unspoken the therapist can do little directly to help the client with it. I do not think that I try to be especially alert to the thoughts of suicide, but the fact that my client may be considering taking his or her own life does sometimes occur to me during therapy. I am more likely to think of it with clients who have been speaking of certain things: of thoughts of pain, loneliness, and perhaps revenge. When the thought does come to me, I speak it aloud without waiting for the client to do so. I am not afraid of putting the idea into his head. This seems to me a distinctly minor danger, if one at all. I am much more concerned with the fact that he has the idea in his head but is keeping it from me because of his embarrassment or concern over how I would react. Just as I noted in Chapter 6 that I am not afraid of mentioning the possibility of a client being crazy, I am not afraid to say that he or she might sometimes think of taking his own life. After all, my client in therapy is asked to risk speaking of whatever comes to his mind, and for his sake, I must be willing to do the same.

Extreme Breaks with Reality

Although this book (for reasons explained in Chapter 14) is not much concerned with diagnosis, a chapter on emergencies must consider those extreme breaks with reality which are sometimes called "psychotic breaks." In a relatively short amount of time the client seems to have lost a common view of the world on which we depend to get through life. If the client is living in an environment which will tolerate this, and if he or she does not seem to be a physical danger to herself or to others, I believe that hospitalization is not a good idea. Hospitalization runs too great a risk of confirming to the client that she is someone who is hopelessly ill. It is unfortunate that this is the meaning of psychiatric hospitalization, but the fact is that it is often thus perceived. Sometimes, though, measures must be taken which go beyond the range of psychotherapy. The following example is an illustration of this.

While on the staff of a large state hospital, one of the in-patients I saw in therapy was a woman in her twenties who had been officially diagnosed as schizophrenic. During the first month or so of our therapy, she seemed to improve greatly. What the ward staff had noted as her delusions and hallucinations seemed to stop. She seemed to be making realistic plans for leaving the hospital. About this time, she became involved in a romantic affair with another hospital patient. I was away from the hospital on a brief vacation during the time when the affair grew rapidly in intensity and then ended with a severe breakdown on the part of the other patient (due to factors too complex to mention here, but apparently no more than partially related to the relationship between them). In the second therapy session after I returned to the hospital, my client began to tell me that she was afraid that she would take her own life. She told me that she did not want to die, but that some force within her seemed to be urging her to kill herself. She pleaded that psychotherapy was not enough in her desperate fear that this force would overwhelm her when she was alone. She had some sophisticated and accurate knowledge of hospital treatment from her professional background as well as her experience as a client, and she begged to be given electro-convulsive therapy. I have some bias against shock treatment, as do many psychologists, but its occasional overuse and misuse do not change the fact that it is sometimes empirically effective. I spoke to the psychiatrist in charge of her ward and a course of electro-convulsive therapy was begun. I continued to see her during this time and after the shock treatment. The compulsive suicidal urges did seem to pass as a result of the electric shock treatment, and therapy seemed to continue to be helpful in terms of her overall picture of herself and her world. Within a few months she was able to leave the hospital, and when I last heard news of her, a couple of years after her discharge, she was still outside a hospital.

Most of the problems associated with the onset of "crazy" thoughts and troubles with reality contact can, however, be handled totally within psychotherapy. If the therapist has a genuine, warm feeling for the client, and the client has been able to perceive this at times, they are likely to be able to continue working usefully together. The most important thing is for the therapist not to be badly thrown off by the client's "symptoms." If the client's language becomes strange and hard to follow, if at times she does not seem to make sense in the way she did before, the therapist must not give up.

I work on the faith that my client is still trying to communicate with me, and that if I listen carefully I will, with her help, be able to understand her communications. Eugene Gendlin (1967) has written an excellent paper describing his style of interacting with clients who have trouble communicating. It is important to read it in its original form in order to get the sensitive, alive feeling which is the heart of it. Among its main points are Gendlin's refusal to give up trying to communicate no matter what the client's attitude seems to be, and Gendlin's willingness to guess wrongly about the client's feelings in the effort to make those feelings clearer to both of them.

A sudden increase in the severity of a client's symptoms, an apparent difficulty in keeping contact with reality, may be caused by various stresses in and around the client. It is important for the therapist to consider the possibility that a key stress might arise from something going wrong in the course of psychotherapy. Is there something in the therapy interaction which is putting added strain on the client? I ask the client if this might be so, and try to ask in an open and nonpunitive, nondefensive way. If no response is received, I try to suggest aloud possible sources of such stress. "Perhaps I have been pushing too hard here; maybe I have not been respecting your right to feel bad once in a while and have just been insisting too damn hard that you get well in a hurry to please me." Or another possibility: "Maybe I have been missing something important you tried to say to me; maybe there is something you have said again and again in a way that you wanted me to hear, and I have just not been able to hear it. If something like that is happening, I guess you might react with pretty strong feelings. Maybe sadness, despair, anger—I just don't know for sure, but I do want to understand better what is going on now." The therapist had better be prepared for the possibility of much hostility being directed against him. And, in accordance with my sixth client perception that the client is the final judge of his or her own feelings, the therapist had better be prepared to treat such hostility as a real and justified product of what the client has perceived in the relationship between them. Perhaps it will turn out to be an important misperception on the part of the client, but any defensiveness on the part of the therapist will keep that misperception from being cleared up. Rather than looking first for an error on the part of the client, it is better to ask yourself and your client, "What might I have done or said that could reasonably be viewed as irritating or anger-provoking?"

Hospitalization and Drug Therapy: Special Problems for the Nonphysician Therapist

Sometimes a client does have to be hospitalized. Sometimes he does present an immediate physical danger to himself or others. Sometimes he does not live in a home environment which will tolerate unusual behavior. At such times a psychotherapist who is also a physician with a hospital affiliation can deal directly with the family, the client, and the hospital to arrange for the client's admission. Perhaps there is no family to be contacted; the physician will then arrange directly through his or her hospital connections for the admission. The procedures for such psychiatric admission should, of course, be well known to him.

It seems to me very wise for the nonphysician therapist to have a good working relationship with a physician who has hospital affiliations in the area. Often the physician will be a psychiatrist, although this is not always mandatory. In addition, the therapist should be familiar with the emergency hospitalization procedures available. Frequently this involves a county hospital. A meeting with the hospital psychiatrist will help clarify these important issues.

Another special problem for the nonphysician therapist is the use of psycho-active drugs, tranquilizers and activators, during the course of psychotherapy. Such drugs seem unnecessary for the activity of psychotherapy itself, though by reducing the amount of obvious anxiety in the client they may make the inexperienced therapist feel more comfortable (Karon & O'Grady, 1969). These chemical adjuncts to psychotherapy may, though, sometimes help a client through stressful periods of living. They must, of course, be dispensed by a knowledgeable physician. Here, again, a good working relationship with an M.D. is important for the nonphysician psychotherapist. In addition to this, the therapist should make himself familiar with the primary action and side effects of any drugs his client may be taking. A good printed source of such information is the *Physician's Desk Reference*, published annually by Medical Economics, Inc., Oradell, New Jersey, which can supplement the information the therapist gets from the client's physician.

Emergency Telephone Calls

One evening, about 8 o'clock, I was called at home from one of the University's dormitories. "Hello, Dr. Kramer, this is Margaret. You remember, you saw me a few days ago in your office." I remembered. She had come looking for psychotherapy, and because our clinic schedule was very full and she had the financial resources to go elsewhere I had recommended private psychotherapy. She told me she had an appointment with her therapist the next day, but she was feeling very lonely and afraid at the moment. She said that she had been unable to reach her therapist and had called me. I talked with her for about 15 or 20 minutes, trying to understand the feeling she was having, and by the end of the conversation she said she was feeling much better. When she had been in my office a few days before, she had talked about suicide and that was one of the main reasons I had given her my home phone number. She did not talk about it in this conversation, but I was still concerned. I asked her to telephone me again about 10 o'clock.

At just 10 o'clock the phone rang. I picked it up and a very small, high, frightened voice said, "Hello, this is Margie. I don't know who you are, but I promised to call you at 10 o'clock. I'm a very good girl, so I called you, and I'm not bad like everybody says." I tried to get Margaret, now shrunken back in her own mind to little Margie, to talk with me about her feelings. She only kept telling me that she was a good girl, but that everyone including her father thought that she was bad. That made her feel so bad and alone that she was going to take some pills she had and then she would be dead and no one would pick on her anymore. I asked her where she was calling from. "I don't know." I asked her what she could see from where she was. "I'm in a telephone booth, and there are a lot of big girls standing around who want to use the telephone." And then she hung up the phone.

I guessed from the description that she was still at the dormitory. I finally got the House Mother of the dormitory on the telephone. I like to respect a client's privacy and right to confidentiality, but now it was a matter of life and death for a person who seemed unable to judge adequately what her own actions meant. By the time the House Mother and several dorm residents had gotten to Margaret, she had already taken a handful of various sorts of pills. She was taken immediately to a nearby hospital, where her stomach was pumped. The timing was close, but action had been taken quickly enough so that she recovered from her suicide attempt.

If a client comes to my office who seems in any danger of making a suicide attempt or of having a kind of break with reality, I give him or her all the telephone numbers at which I can be reached. I tell him that if I'm not there, he should leave a message saying where he can be reached and how late and I will call back as soon as I can. Of course, I cannot be certain when I have such a client, so I try to be very careful to err in my judgment on the generous side only.

A few general points may be illustrated with the above telephone calls from Margaret. First, as noted, I saw to it that she had my phone number available. Second, when she did call me I did not take it simply as a signal to make an appointment to see her later. Had she not had an appointment with another psychotherapist already planned, I would have made plans to see her myself, but this still would not have discharged my responsibility to her. If someone calls a therapist, she is troubled now and wants help now. A psychotherapy session by telephone is not as clear, as satisfying, or generally as long as a psychotherapy session in the office. Still, however, it can be a period of sharing between client and therapist. It still can be a genuine interaction in which the therapist makes his or her own self, concern, warmth, and respect apparent to the client. I tried to do that in my first phone call with Margaret. I thought I had been effective and helpful to her, but I still asked that she call again. This is the third point to be made here. I generally ask the client to phone me again at some specified time; occasionally if more convenient, I promise to call him or her back at some set time. Both are indications to her of my wanting to be helpful, and of the fact that my desire to be helpful does not end when the telephone connection is severed. I have a feeling that the period between one call and the next is a time when, in a sense, I am with the client in her perceptions even though we are not together. I am not so strongly with her as when we are actually talking, but I think I am more strongly there than I would be in the stretch between a single phone call and the next appointment. The "two phone call approach" thus stretches out the effective length of the telephone psychotherapy session.

Sometimes the suicide call comes even later than Margaret's. Lillian was an unmarried client of mine who had recently discovered she was pregnant. Her boyfriend knew of this, but she had hidden the news from her family. She had made arrangements for what appeared to be a medically safe abortion, though it was not through legal channels. I did not, of course, attempt in any way to stand in judgment on the legality or morality of the procedures. I received a phone call from her in the middle of the weekend. Tearfully, she told me that she had not gone for the planned abortion that day but instead had stayed in her room where she had just taken an overdose of tranquilizers. I urged her to call the police immediately; in that city they could be relied upon to take rapid measures for emergency hospitalization. I probably spoke somewhat harshly to her, because I felt an edge of panic and guilt myself; I had in no way foreseen that this might happen. I made sure that she knew the emergency police number, and I asked her to phone me back as soon as she called them. Ten minutes passed without a call from her. I phoned her apartment, and the police were already there. The officer who had answered the telephone asked me for the name and address of Lillian's parents, which she had declined to give. I responded that she was over 21, and that I had to legally respect her rights to confidentiality with me and could not share with them the information she chose to withhold. The officer was courteous and assured me that he understood my position. He reassured me that she was still conscious and moving about, and he let me speak with her for a few moments before the emergency ambulance took her to the hospital. One of the officers apparently took care to see that the receiving hospital got my name when she came in, so that when I called to inquire about her condition they had heard of me and knew that I was her psychotherapist.

Because of hospital requirements, it eventually became necessary for her family to know of her condition and the events preceding it. I wonder now if perhaps she really wanted them to know. Perhaps I had been missing some communication in psychotherapy, which if received would have eliminated the need for her to take such drastic steps in calling her condition to the world's attention. I do not know for sure, and I cannot know. Psychotherapy is not a good profession for people who must be certain. It is often a lonely profession. Lillian had arrived at the hospital in time; she survived, and there were no serious after-effects from the pills she had taken.

In this example, the emergency nature of the situation prevented my trying to offer psychotherapy by telephone. I still suspect that I could have been more open and empathic even in my hasty advice to call the police. Perhaps if I had been so, she would have telephoned me back. It is worth noting here the interest and courtesy shown by the police. Whether we tend to be primarily supporters or attackers of the local police, they are usually people who understand the concept of an emergency. My dealings with the police in this kind of connection have, it is true, been few, but they typically brought me into contact with policemen who were fast-acting, concerned, and courteous regarding the professional problems involved.

This concludes the chapter on "Emergencies." The next chapter is one dealing with client's relatives; another illustration of a phone call opens the chapter.

13

The Client's Relatives

I had seen Alex for only two sessions of psychotherapy before the phone call came. His voice on the phone sounded heavy and blurred. I thought I could identify in it the sounds of sadness, alcohol, and perhaps other drugs. Alex was in his mid-twenties and lived at home with his parents. He told me now that he was terribly frightened, and that he had been drinking too much and was unable to stop (one of the problems which had brought him to therapy), and that he was afraid that his father would throw him out of the house. He told me that his father wanted to talk to me. "Please talk to him, please," Alex pleaded. I agreed, and Alex screamed out to his father to get on the phone. After he had spoken only a few words, Alex's voice cut through again. His father immediately ordered him to get off the phone and let the two of us talk without interruption. I cut in quickly before Alex could reply.

"I don't want you to interrupt us now, Alex," I told him. "I don't have any secrets from you, so I'm glad to have you listen while your father and I talk. You're my client, and I can't be helpful to you unless I can be completely open with you. But I want to ask you to be quiet now so that I can hear what your father has to say. Stay with us, but let us talk now."

The father began to describe his son's behavior and his deep concern about what was happening to him. Again, Alex's voice cut in. At first, his father said, "Now, you get off . . ." Then he remembered what I had said to Alex for both of them to hear, and he changed it to, "Stay on the phone, Alex, but let me talk to the doctor now." As he spoke, it became clear that he was not planning to throw his son out of the house. Perhaps such threats had been made in the past, but that was not the current situation. Now he was only asking Alex to please go to bed and "try to sleep it off." Alex came in again with his fears of being thrown out and his fears of what was happening to him. The three of us talked together for just a few minutes, but I had the feeling that Alex and his father began to hear each other a little better and more accurately than they had before the call began. I suggested that we might want to all get together in person sometime, that Alex and I would talk about the possibility more when he and I got together at our next session. The father agreed that it might be a good idea, and the call ended there.

The need to work actively with the client's relatives comes up relatively rarely in psychotherapy with adults. Because it does sometimes arise, though, I want to give a short chapter dealing with it here. As noted in Chapter Two, however, this is mainly a book about the one-to-one relationship in individual psychotherapy. Family therapy, couples therapy, marriage counseling are all important areas, but they are fields of their own and not the main subject of this book. This chapter, then, makes no claims to completeness. It is only a series of notes on certain aspects of dealing with the client's family.

Two Aspects of Confidentiality

The telephone call described above illustrates an important point about confidentiality which should be made clear to clients and their families. Most clients understand that what they say to you will be held in confidence. It is still worth telling that to your client, particularly in the case of young clients who are most likely to doubt it, but most of them understand it. The other aspect of confidentiality is less widely understood but is just as important. While I will keep all of my client's communications secret (if he or she wishes me to), no one else may have any secrets with me about him. I cannot allow any other person to tell me anything about my client which I cannot share with him. This would violate the kind of openness and mutual respect which must go on between us. I not only have to resist the pressure of relatives who wish to tell me things in confidence, I have to be careful to resist my own temptation to try to uncover facts before my client chooses to share them. It might seem nice and curiosity-satisfying at times to ask my client's mother or my client's wife some fact about him that he is not ready to share with me. But if I cannot wait until he is ready to trust me with the important things about himself, or if he never does come to trust me with them, then I cannot help him. Psychotherapy does not operate effectively on the basis of an accumulation of facts and information. The only really useful facts and information are those which grow out of a trusting relationship. When I talked with Alex and his father on the telephone, I tried to make clear to them that I could keep no secrets from Alex if useful psychotherapy was to be done. His father, fortunately, understood my message quickly. He also made the choice of continuing to speak openly with me, even though Alex would hear, rather than refusing to speak with me at all. Not every relative makes the same choice.

I always welcome the chance to explain the issues of confidentiality in the presence of both the client and a member of his family (in the case of children, I consider it essential to say it out loud in the presence of both child and parent). I want each of them to know that the other has gotten the message too. Another useful aspect of talking to client and relative together is that it may help them to communicate with each other. Something of this took place in the phone call with Alex and his father. Somehow, by the end of the call, they seemed to have heard and understood each other better. This kind of improved communication is often the goal of the occasional session with the client and his or her parent, or the client and spouse.

Sometimes a telephone call comes from a father or mother, and the client is nowhere around. Mother is calling, perhaps, to find out how her 25-year-old daughter is doing in psychotherapy and also to let you know some things about the daughter that she might not have gotten around to telling you. When this kind of call comes, I try to announce my rules as quickly as possible. As soon as I recognize my caller, I interrupt and say something like, "Excuse me for interrupting you, Mrs. Blank, but I really feel I must explain something to you before I let you tell me anything more about your daughter. You know, of course, that whatever your daughter says to me is confidential between us, and I can't share any of that with you. What I also want to explain is that I can't keep any secrets from your daughter. Anything you tell me in the conversation, I'll share with her. I don't know if that seems unusual to you or not, but I've found that that's the only way I can really be helpful in psychotherapy." Some psychotherapists refuse to listen to such telephone messages. I have some sympathy for that position—in a way, it makes life easier—but if a parent still wants to talk to me after I explain that I will not keep the message secret, I have sometimes found it useful to listen. The usefulness seems to be in opening communication channels between parent and son or daughter. The knowledge that I will share everything said to me with my client sometimes makes the parent more willing to be directly open with my client as well. It is as if Mother calls me and wants to tell me a secret; I make it clear that I will not keep secrets, but she wants to tell it so badly that she says it anyway. Then, since she knows it is no longer a secret, she says it directly to her daughter, too. Of course, it does not always work this way, but it sometimes does and it is a helpful thing when it happens.

Naturally, not all parents are equally receptive to my rules. As a rough generalization, parents who are paying for their child's psychotherapy are more likely to feel that they have special privileges with the psychotherapist than if the client were paying. Another major factor that seems to operate in deciding how well the parents will accept my notions of confidentiality and openness is whether they regard my client as a young child. This may not bear any very close relationship to the client's chronological age. I remember seeing a 12-year-old boy who was regarded by his mother as virtually an adult, and she correspondingly respected his independence in psychotherapy. She knew his rights to confidentiality and never expected to have a special relationship with me simply because her son was in therapy. On the other hand, I remember a 28-year-old woman who was regarded by her parents as a very young child. They treated her like a child at home, worried about whether or not she would take the right bus and come home on time, and correspondingly expected that they could have private conversations with me about their girl. They felt that adults had the right to discuss children without the children knowing. They were not pleased when I explained that I could not do things their way.

I remember a situation where I was not sufficiently sensitive to this sort of thing. I had had only two or three sessions with a client, a man of 18. I had met his mother and talked with them together at his first session, so I did have some sense that she still regarded him as a baby. I had, of course, explained my rules about confidentiality and the fact that I would not keep any secrets from him. Before our scheduled fourth session, his mother called to tell me that he would be unable to come in at the scheduled time. I said that I wanted to talk with him myself to work out a time. He came to the phone and we arranged a new appointment. The day of that appointment, his mother called in the morning and said he would be unable to come in but that she would phone me again to set up a new appointment. She never did call me again. A year later I discovered by chance what had happened. She had been incensed by the fact that I had set up the appointment with the client himself rather than with her. After all, he was only a baby and she was paying for his psychotherapy. She certainly had no intention of paying a therapist who would talk to her son rather than to her concerning grown-up matters like setting appointments. Looking back over this incident, I feel that if I had been more sensitive to what was going on, I might have been able to say something which would have clarified the situation. Perhaps I could have explained that treating her son like a grown-up was an important part of psychotherapy, and she might have been able to accept this well enough to let him continue in treatment with me.

Joint Sessions—and Who Suggests Them

Sometimes it is the client himself who suggests that the therapist see a relative. This can come about in many different ways and for many different reasons. Sometimes a client has asked me to see his mother or father so that I could be of help to the parent. Sometimes this seems to be because the client has assigned himself the task of being a parent to his parent. He has taken on himself the burden and responsibility of protecting his parents and helping them to change. Perhaps he wants my help in how to do this, or perhaps he wants me to do it directly so that the responsibility will be taken away from him. When I think this is the case, I try to say something like: "I can't help your mother. I'm not her psychotherapist. That's not my job. My job is with you. Your mother matters to me, is important to me in a way, because she is important to you. But she's not my client; you are." I may also go on to explain that not only isn't helping his mother my job, but teaching him how to help his mother is also not my main job. He hired me to help him to grow, not to help him to help someone else.

Sometimes a client wants to bring in a relative—a parent or spouse—just to show you what he is up against. He wants you to see that his wife, or his mother or father is really as bad as he says. He is looking for an ally. One of the clear signs of this kind of situation is when the client says something like, "I'd like it if my dad and I could come in together here sometime, but you better watch him carefully because he can act really charming when he first meets somebody and wants to make a good impression." The client is already cautioning me that I had better not be taken in, and I had better remember that it is he and I together against his father. The therapist should also be aware that a client's suggestion that a relative really be seen in person can indicate concern about the therapist's empathy. It may be a way of saying: "You are not sensitive enough to really understand the kind of person and situation I have been describing to you; I had better bring the person here in an effort to get through to you and show you what I am up against."

Frequently, an occasional joint session is a good thing. If my client really wants me to see his mother or his wife, I am willing to do this for one of our sessions together. Probably my client wants, in part at least, to get my reaction to the relative. I assure him that I cannot know nearly as much from seeing his mother once as he knows about her from having grown up with her. Often, however, I learn something about their interaction which he may have missed and which I can share with him. I have also sometimes found that a client is then more comfortable and open in talking about some person I have actually met than about someone I have heard of exclusively from him.

Sometimes it is a relative or a close friend of the client who initiates the request for a joint session. Perhaps my client's wife would like to really see the mysterious psychotherapist. Perhaps she has her own half-formed fantasies about the man who is "giving advice" to her husband about how to change. One or two sessions is not much chance for her to form an opinion about me, but if the client is open to her coming then let her have that chance. It may help make communication between the two of them better. When they are both with me, I will comment as best I can on their style of communicating with each other. I will also try to answer questions about myself which a visiting relative may have.

I do not, however, answer questions about my client. The client's right to confidentiality is as strongly respected during joint sessions as at any other time. It is this essential regard for the client's privacy which puts a clamp on how useful occasional joint sessions can be. Unless my client is willing to be as fully and completely open with another person as I ask him to try to be with me, important areas of his life cannot be discussed at these times. In joint sessions I focus on the here-and-now interactions among the three of us. A guiding principle for the therapist in joint sessions is: *Watch what you say!* If you let slip material which your client has told you in confidence, you will quite rightly lose his trust in you. You may notice something about the visiting relative or the client's interaction with her which seems importantly relevant to things you and the client have talked of before. *Save it.* Remember it, or write yourself a note about it, and talk about it at the next session when just you and your client are together again, without a third person.

It is not only parents and spouses who come into such sessions. I remember a client of mine, a woman in her early forties, whose daughter wanted very much to meet her mother's "shrink." The mother and I agreed that this was a reasonable curiosity. We were also able to see, especially when the three of us got together, that it was a kind of curiosity which showed greater caring and involvement between mother and daughter than my client had realized existed. I have also, at times, invited a friend of the client's to join us. Bernard Steinzor, a therapist with a rationale similar to mine in these issues, sometimes initiates the joint session himself (Steinzor, 1967, pp. 26–37):

> During recent years I have indicated directly to a patient who was engaged or married and occasionally even just going steady that I was ready to meet his close friend, if the patient and friend wished this. I justify this suggestion simply on the basis of the friend's understandable curiosity. How can he be a friend and not be curious about the doctor? I indicate that I will not enter into any discussion about any ongoing fracas or pleasures between them unless they ask.

I recall a time when I was much more hesitant about this sort of thing myself, and a client asked if he could bring his steady "girl friend" to a session. I said that it did not seem quite appropriate to me. He asked me if I occasionally saw a husband and wife together, and I admitted that I did. "Well, then," he demanded, "If I go out and marry her, then can I bring her here one time?" I got the point—the closeness and importance of a relationship is not determined by legal contract—and I saw the two of them together without demanding a wedding license.

Thus, I am available to be seen and inspected—if my client wants it—by parent or offspring, spouse or friend. Who I am in psychotherapy is not a secret issue; I have never asked my client to avoid speaking about me or our psychotherapy. It is his rights to privacy which have to be respected. When he wants to have me help him reveal our private interaction a bit and let some part of it be seen by someone close to him, I am ready and willing to oblige.

14

Traditional Issues: Diagnosis, Transference, and Exploring the Past

Three issues are dealt with in this chapter: the importance of diagnosis for therapy, transference in psychotherapy, and the importance of exploring the client's past. In some schemes of practicing psychotherapy, each of these plays an important part. They do not play as major a role in the view of psychotherapy set forth in this book. The aim of this chapter is to show what part they do play and why it is a smaller one.

The Importance of Diagnosis

Diagnostic or classification schemes may be set up for "pure" scientific purposes or for their direct implications for clinical practice and treatment. The pure scientific purposes never conflict with application, but neither do they necessarily serve the purposes of applied science in any direct fashion. Kraepelin, whose nineteenth century psychiatric classifications still influence us, was looking for the scientifically true and valid mental disorders. The model he probably had in mind stemmed from the successes of nineteenth century bacteriologists such as Pasteur and Koch. This simple concept of disease states roughly that one first recognizes a syndrome or collection of symptoms which always occur together. Correct identification of the syndrome then leads to the underlying cause of the disease (just as Koch moved from recognized syndromes to the discovery of the disease producing bacteria under his microscope). Then the hope and belief is that with the causative agent discovered, the cure is only a short step away. But this simple disease model will not serve for the kinds of mental and emotional disorders covered in this book. Even the first step, the identification of the syndrome, seems to fall down.

The *Diagnostic and Statistical Manual of the American Psychiatric Association* (American Psychiatric Association, 1968) gives brief syndrome descriptions of the various "mental disorders." The expected collection of symptoms for such things as "paranoid schizophrenia," "passive aggressive personality," and so forth, are described. The presumption is that psychiatrists, perhaps with the amplified knowledge derived from available textbooks and clinical practice, can identify the "diseases" so described. But it does not seem to happen that way. A number of studies have been done to investigate how much psychiatrists can agree on the diagnosis of a given client or a set of clients, and the results have not been encouraging. Only the very broadest categories—psychosis, neurosis, and sometimes personality disorders—can be agreed upon considerably better than chance, although there is still quite a bit of disagreement present. Finer distinctions into type of psychosis or type of neurosis seem hopelessly scattered as various psychiatrists disagree with each other while examining the same clients (Kreitman, 1961; Kreitman, Sainsbury, Morrissey, Towers, & Scrivner, 1961). Even the broad categories seem somewhat unreliable. A study was done in two major Naval hospitals comparing the diagnosis of clients when admitted with their diagnosis at discharge (Arthur & Gunderson, 1966). At one of the hospitals only 18 percent of those who entered with a diagnosis of neurotic were discharged with some sort of neurotic label still used to describe them (i.e., they were not discharged as "normal," but some non-neurotic psychiatric category had been assigned to them). At the other hospital, 37 percent of the clients originally called psychoneurotic—still well under half—were still judged as belonging to that category rather than to some other at the time of discharge. At one hospital, 38 percent of the clients diagnosed as psychotic had the same admission and discharge diagnosis, while at the other only 22 percent did. When the authors examined the nature of the changes in psychiatric labeling, they concluded that, "changes in diagnosis were thought to be contributable to a combination of client characteristics and administrative dispositional policies rather than changes in the clinical status of the clients" (p. 144). In other words, the change in diagnosis between admission and discharge seemed to have very little to do with the clinical state of the clients; it had to do with other things going on in the hospital. The treatment styles and skills seemed to be much the same at both hospitals, and the clients or patients in each were similar. The hospitals differed in their way of administering psychiatric labels.

To sum up, then, our present standard set of diagnostic labels seems impossible to apply with any regularity based on the conditions of our clients. Some attempts to get more reliably recognizable syndromes are being made. The work of Lorr and his associates is a good example (Lorr, Klett, & McNair, 1963). This work, based on close and detailed observation and classification of behavior, may lead to new treatment paths as well as more reliable syndromes, but at this point in its development the outcome is still uncertain.

"Diagnosis is a design for action" (Cameron, 1953). This is part of the ideal of diagnosis set up in an article by Cameron in a symposium on current problems in psychiatric diagnosis (Hoch & Zubin, 1953). Cameron also recognized, however, that our present diagnostic categories were far from meeting that ideal. In fact, it is possible to be seriously misled in one's design for action by current concepts of diagnosis. I remember a client at a University clinic whom I saw a couple of years ago. When he first walked into my office for the intake interview it was clear he was extremely tense. His facial muscles and body posture were held rigidly. He sat down and began by saying he had talked with a lot of people about his problems, about his tensions and his worries, and now he had come to see a psychologist. I told him that it seemed to me that if he had talked to so many people already he must have something special that he felt he could only say to a psychologist.

Why didn't he begin by saying it now? "I can't ever relax," he said. "Like, you see, my feet," pointing down to his black shoes, "If I were to relax them now the black from the shoes would enter my body and poison it."

He then related a few other symptoms which together with the first would easily earn him the formal diagnosis of schizophrenic in most professional circles. In many of these circles the implications for action following such a labeling would be that such a person would have to be seen very frequently and over a very long period of time for any help to be accomplished. In the University setting where I saw him, with its many practical limitations, I arranged for our interviews to occur twice a week and occasionally only once a week. The delusional material which he had brought in had largely passed by the fifteenth interview. By the thirtieth interview we terminated therapy. The "schizophrenic" symptoms had not returned over a year later. When I saw the young man at that time he was taking a temporary leave from the University, but not because of any difficulties or inabilities. He had obtained permission to use his scholoarship for a year abroad, and had been accepted by a university there. Had I believed in a too simple and compelling set of connections between symptom and labeling and prognosis, my prejudices in this matter might well have kept me from being able to help.

There is some research evidence to suggest that some therapists work better than others with clients labeled as "schizophrenic." This research (Betz, 1967) has discovered ways of identifying such therapists by means of a psychological test, although such identifications are by no means perfect. It is not at all clear how such therapists work differently with clients than do others.

My experience has led me to believe that the principles described in this book are true for "schizophrenic" clients as well as "neurotic" ones. Some research has tended to confirm this point, though it is by no means fully established (Marshall, 1977). The "necessary perceptions" I have described in Chapter 5 seem to me neither more nor less important in my interactions with clients who have been called "schizophrenic." I believe that the differences are in a differing ability of therapists to have a sense of respect and empathy for these clients and to communicate these qualities to them.

Perhaps some of us have a greater gift than others for knowing what it feels like to be "crazy." I can suggest a couple of books which seem to me so vivid and real in their presentation of the schizophrenic world as to be of use to a therapist who wants to increase his understanding of what this means. One of them is the novel *I Never Promised You A Rose Garden* (Green, 1965). Under the thinnest disguise of fiction, the book is a description of the author's psychosis, hospitalization, and recovery with the help of a skilled and sensitive psychotherapist. Another book is the *Diary of Vaslav Nijinsky* (Nijinsky, 1968), the strange and deeply moving journal which the great Russian dancer kept during the years immediately preceding his final psychiatric hospitalization. One of the most sensitive and clearly presented accounts of trying to work with such clients is the paper by Gendlin (1967) which has already been mentioned in a similar connection in Chapter 12.

As a psychologist, I feel that something should be said about psychological testing. To the extent that psychological testing is aimed at formal diagnostic categories, it is subject to all the difficulties that have been listed. It arrives at a label about which there will be limited agreement and which has no clear and reliable implications for action. In certain settings, however, testing is potentially of value. When there are not enough therapists to provide help to all who apply to a clinic setting, testing may help to identify those who most urgently need it at that very time. It may also—though I am not certain of this—identify those who can profit most from it.

The psychological testing report, itself, may provide a first, semi-impressionistic step toward a meaningful concept of "diagnosis." The good, potential-using test report presents a picture of a real human being whom the psychologist-tester has encountered. While the formal label with which the report sometimes closes may not be helpful, the reactions of another person to the client now before you may be of some aid in understanding him. It may help the client, too, in understanding himself. If a client of mine has been given psychological tests, I share with him the material in the report. I share it with him in the language he and I use with each other rather than in the formal language of the psychologist. But I do this for the sake of clarity, not in order to hide things from him.

Before closing these notes on diagnosis, I want to share a fantasy of mine about relabeling our categories of emotional problems. As I noted earlier in this chapter, the only categories which psychiatrists can recognize reliably are the broad ones of neurosis, psychosis, and personality disorder. I suggest these three be relabeled respectively as *nervous, crazy,* and *odd.* First of all, these have the advantages of being common English words without a mass of untestable theory and supposition behind them. And they do fit the main characteristics of the traditional syndromes. Neurotics are supposedly characterized mainly by anxiety—or nervousness. Psychotics are those who seem "crazy" in the popular sense—out of touch with what most of us recognize as our shared realities. And the so-called personality disorders are those persons who seem strange or odd to some of us, without being much bothered by it themselves. My system of "nervous, crazy, odd" would also help settle the issue of whether someone can have multiple diagnoses or not. The question of whether someone can be both neurotic and psychotic seems like a difficult and profound issue. The answer to whether someone can be both nervous and crazy is an obvious "yes." Those qualities can exist either separately or together in the same person.

Another issue clarified by my system is that we may not have the same right to try to treat or "change" persons in each category. If someone is primarily "nervous," the issue is probably clear. He or she wants relief from that discomfort and has probably come willingly for help. If a person is mainly "crazy," we can bet that being out of contact with our best notions of reality causes severe problems in living. At some level, this person, too, probably wants our help. But what about someone who is mainly "odd"? What right do we have to try to impose ordinariness upon the odd? In connection with this, note who does the labeling (or name-calling) in each case. The "nervous" person would readily agree to being called nervous. The crazy person may or may not agree to being crazy. (Most, by the way, will agree at times—partly because no one seems to be crazy all over all the time.) But the label "odd" (just like the label "personality disorder") is one that is nearly always imposed from outside the person; it is the label we "normals" impose upon someone whom we feel should be more like us. These are the persons who are sent by others for "treatment," rather than seeking it for themselves. They come as court referrals or school referrals or under pressure from a relative. If someone's oddness has not made him or her notably nervous or crazy, what right do we have as psychotherapists to intervene? I am afraid that such intervention may make the therapist primarily an enforcer of social conformity in such cases. And that is a role that I do not happily accept.

Transference in Psychotherapy

In psychoanalysis "transference" is most accurately used to describe certain feelings which the client has toward the therapist. These are feelings which the client once held toward previous significant figures in his life, and they are not appropriate to the real personality of the therapist and the client's current relationship to him. Freud particularly used the term "transference" to refer to the powerful attachments to parents or parent-like figures. These residues from childhood are often mixtures of strong, sexualized love, plus resentment and even hate. I, myself, believe that each of us brings to any new, important relationship a collection of hopes, expectations, and fears. The client who comes to see me does have a history of parents, teachers, friends, and enemies: a history which will affect his or her initial view of all new involvements, including the one with me. Such "distortions" are not, of course, limited to therapy relationships. Freud himself (Freud, 1915) has pointed out the strong similarities between "transference love" and the "genuine love" which makes its appearance outside of analytic treatment.

Here is a short section of therapy in which something like a transference type distortion does occur. The client is speaking of her mother. The therapist and client are both women. The client is about 40; the therapist somewhat younger.

> C: I was very small, and one time my mother and I were down visiting my aunt—the one that lives in _____ now. We were visiting her, and my mother wanted to go down to Sears to shop, and I didn't want her to go, and my aunt offered me something very enticing . . . as a bribe, shall we say, to get me to accept the idea of my mother going. They had this old typewriter that I just loved. I was very fascinated with the typewriter and with the piano, because I used to play the piano even though I couldn't play; I used to enjoy fooling around with the piano when I was at my aunt's house—she had one of those big old upright players, and she offered to let me play with that typewriter, which was enticing, in exchange for my mother going to Sears for a little while. And do you know, as enticing as that was, I still didn't want my mother to go . . . and leave me there . . . with my aunt. I did not want to be away from my mother for a minute.
>
> T: [quietly]: You still don't.
>
> C: Hmm. [long pause] Aah! [long pause]

T: Can you tell me what you're experiencing right now?

C: Ohh. [*pause*] Ahh. [*pause*] Wow . . . That remark hit me just like a ton of bricks. [*pause*] Two things . . . Fear and sadness . . . Fear because I realized that what you said was true . . . hit me very suddenly. Sadness because I know it's not possible. So . . . I have felt this way for years . . . but I . . . I wasn't aware of the fact that . . . until you made that remark that this was indeed true. . . . But why do I feel that way?

T: What comes to mind?

C: I don't know . . . I don't know . . . I don't know . . . it's very difficult to explain; there is more to it than what I just said. That was the general feeling, but, um . . . it's a very strange thing to say. It almost seemed that for a second, for a very fraction of a second . . . *you turned into my mother* . . . Somehow. . . . I can't explain it . . . You didn't look like her or anything physically in any way, but somehow you turned into my mother for a second a few minutes ago. I can't explain it. I don't know how . . . I don't know how to explain it. . . . I can't explain it because I don't know why it happened or—ah, it was just almost really like a thunderbolt hit me . . . That's just what—was like a sensation; something hit me real hard . . . Ahh . . . by that remark . . . and—and that—I felt those feelings that I mentioned, but I also felt *that*, and I felt . . . well, extremely overwhelmed. Suddenly overwhelmed.

Because this therapist is someone who shares herself openly and accurately with her client, the client can perceive that what occurs does not really fit the situation. They can look at what happened together and then, if they wish, refocus on the current, genuine relationship between them. Much of my concern over the traditional use of the transference concept is that it ignores what is really, currently going on between therapist and client. I have deemphasized transference in this book partly because of that danger.

Szasz, who disapproves of some of the uses of the transference concept in analysis, has put into words a very clear statement of a harmful traditional view. He notes that "transference" deals with the question of what is real and what is not real: Transference is not the real relationship. Therefore, in cases where the therapist invokes the term "transference" in his interpretations, the term is not a neutral one. "In these cases there is a conflict of opinion between patient and physician, which is not resolved by examination of the merits of the two views, but rather by the physician's autocratic judgment: his view is correct, and is considered a 'reality': the patient's view is incorrect, and is considered 'transference' " (Szasz, 1963, p. 432). If I think that my client seems to react to me in certain ways which are not bound to the reality of our current situation, I share my view with him. We exchange views and look together at how we see things. Sometimes he comes to agree that a distortion is taking place; sometimes I have to yield on my original judgment; sometimes we have to agree to disagree and move on. I think the transference type of situations are also lowered in intensity and frequency by my required "client perception" that the therapist be honestly and openly himself. The more open the therapist is, the easier it is to quickly identify and clarify distortions in the relationship.

"Counter-transference" is used to identify similar distortions in the therapist's view of his client. Here, again, I believe that the therapist's personal openness and his respect for considering the views of his client operate as correctives to this kind of distortion. If I am seeing the client inaccurately because of my needs and relationships in my past, I will eventually share this with him in some ways. If I can listen openly and respectfully to his response to this, I have a good chance to correct myself.

The traditional corrective for counter-transference is therapy for the therapist. The idea is that the therapist who has gone through a successful therapeutic experience of his own will no longer have unrecognized needs which lead to such distortions. Obviously, this is somewhat overstated. I do think that some therapy experience in the role of client is a good idea for the therapist. At least the experience will give him some notion of what it means and what it feels like to be a client. The experience should enable him to at least avoid those distortions in his view of the therapy relationship which come from having no idea of what the experience of being a client is like. I think that the kind of personal growth which comes from good therapy is worthwhile for the therapist. I do not believe it is always a necessity before a person can become a therapist, can enter into a professional, helping relationship with another.

One of the benefits of supervision for a psychotherapist is that his supervisor may help to point out where the therapist is not clearly perceiving the relationship between himself and the client—whether or not the problem areas are labeled as "transference" or "counter-transference." Talking things over with someone else, whether he is a "supervisor," "consultant," or a peer, may help the therapist to clarify things or perceive them more clearly. Just as the therapist helps the client to perceive more clearly his relationships with others, the supervisor or consultant helps the therapist to examine his relationships with the client. Experienced therapists can often make good use of a colleague in this way.

I want to return to Szasz's interesting article before leaving the subject of transference. He notes that invoking this concept may well serve a defensive function for the therapist. "The patient does not really love or hate the analyst, but someone else. What could be more reassuring? This is why so-called transference interpretations are so easily and so often misused; they provide a ready-made opportunity for putting the patient at arm's length" (Szasz, 1963, p. 438). I personally do not recommend psychotherapy as a profession for those who must keep their clients or "patients" emotionally at arm's length. I feel I must face my client's strong feelings and my own. I do not demand that the client meet my needs—not even (or, maybe, especially not) my needs to feel helpful. But I believe I will be virtually useless as a helper if I am afraid to notice that a client may really care about me and that I may really care about him or her.

Importance of the Past in Psychotherapy

I neither encourage nor discourage clients if they wish to talk about events in their past. If these memories are important to them here and now, they are important to both of us. I do feel that we must talk about the present, but as long as the present is not ignored, then the memory of the past is welcome also. I do not, however, consider it essential.

Perhaps the past does cause the present, but therapy does not work on the basis of causality. A British psychoanalyst, Rycroft (1968), has suggested that classical analysis depends on understanding the client's present communication rather than the historical basis of it. After all, we do not know the real past from our client but only the remembered past. Freud (1935) was led into the error of believing that all his hysterical clients had been seduced in childhood by an adult. When he discovered that this was not a part of their real past but only a part of their remembered past, he recognized that it was the remembered past which was the more important.

In any case, the past cannot be changed. Psychotherapy deals with relationships in the here and now. I try to understand what my client's memory of the past means to him in terms of what we are now experiencing together. I have come to regard the past as a kind of metaphor. When my client speaks of the remembered past, I frequently experience him as talking in a metaphorical way about what is happening now. Setting it within the metaphor of the past serves to make it more bearable. It gives it some distance. Perhaps it also holds out the unrealistic hope of changing the past. I listen openly to the "past" events which are described, but I try to open up the metaphor just as one might interpret a poem. I suggest to my client what I think he may also be saying about his present experiences. This notion applies, for example, to the interpretation of transference. In these terms, finding the "historical" roots of the transference is in fact a way of exploring (perhaps more fully or more safely) the relationship between client and therapist: a relationship which is really taking place now.

I mentioned above that Freud discovered that the "hysterical" women, for example, frequently remembered a seduction by a father or father-like figure even though it had not really taken place. He came to believe that childhood fantasies and conflicts influenced how the past was remembered. It seems to me that the emphasis in psychoanalysis is how the remembered past influences the present. But there is another way of looking at that part of Freud's data. I believe strongly—and my experience of clients seems to confirm this—that it is the present conflicts and struggles that influence how we remember the past. I think each of us sometimes reconstructs the past in terms of our fears and hopes of today. Perhaps it was the anguish and confusion which Freud's "hysterics" were currently involved in which made them recall a symbolic history of seduction. In this sense, I find that my client's current involvements in living influence the "past." The remembered past, as told to me in therapy, is a metaphor for the present.

15

Therapist and Client at Work

This chapter shows an example of therapist and client at work. It is a transcript from a tape recording of a therapy session. The recording of this session, in which I was the therapist, is available from the American Academy of Psychotherapists Tape Library, No. 101, "I Feel Guilty for Something I Don't Believe In." (The title is a quote from the client.) While it is fairly easy to follow on tape, it presents some problems here. The actual sounds of our voices give clues to feelings that the words alone express less well. They also make the simple sense of the dialogue easier to understand. I might have "edited" the material to make it more simply readable, but I decided that to do so would no longer be as honest a picture of what went on. I have, in this chapter, interrupted the words of the session from time to time to comment on what I feel was happening between us. The comments are meant to help point out how some of the principles I have described earlier in this book operate in action; they are also meant to identify some of the thoughts and theories which occurred to me during the session. I have not, though, tried to identify and comment on every possible illustration of such matters. Much of the material, hopefully, speaks for itself. As I noted in Chapter 6, I do not often think consciously about principles or theories during my interaction with a client. The comments I have inserted here are primarily processes and influences heard and identified in retrospect.

It is the third therapy session with a woman in her twenties who is considering separation from her husband. They have two young children. She was in therapy several months previously with another therapist. As a matter of fact, I did some supervision of the student therapist she was seeing. Still, it is only our third session together, and we are still learning how to talk and listen to each other.

C: This is always the hardest part for me, opening up. I don't know where to start.

T: What's it feel like to be sitting here, you know, having just come in and getting ready to start?

C: It makes me feel—it's like, a lot of times I want to talk about something, only it's like I don't want to jump right into the middle of it, but I don't really know how to start talking about that, that thing I want to talk about. It's like, I feel funny if I come in and go "Hi, I'm doing good this week." And I want to talk about this and just, I don't know, just it it makes me feel uncomfortable, like just, it's like I feel like I have to have some format to come in and start. And I know—

T: Very well organized.

C: Right, you know, it goes way back to the the thing of trying to do what I'm supposed to do too so that I will benefit from this as much as much as I can. And I feel that if I don't do it right then I won't benefit, but I know that that's not true.

T: If you were a really good girl you'd know how to start therapy sessions, right?

C: It seems like, it seems like there should be an easy way to do it, you know, for me, and um, it's really not hard I just feel like it is. I feel like, um, I feel like I just can't come in and talk like I'm talking right now. [laughter] I know that I, I know that I can, you know, but I still feel like I can't. I feel like I have to come in and have like my note cards or something, you know, um it makes me feel . . .

T: And you get gypped, Jane. Somebody gave you a rule book that says organize your note cards, but they didn't give you the note cards!

C: [laughter] Yeah, right, right. I think back to that a lot, and I think that's stupid, you know, you know, it's not anywhere near as bad as it used to be. Like I used to just be, I used to like three days before I just come in—what am I gonna talk about? You know, and all week long I'd been thinking about a million things I could a talked about. Now I don't; I think about things, but I don't think about them during the week. I don't think about those are the things. I don't think specifically this is what I want to talk about. I just go about my daily thinking and if I happen to remember something that I thought was important or something that really stuck with me for some reason, I, I try, I like to bring it up in here, but I think that it might relate to something. I don't know.

T: O.K., so why don't you give yourself a few seconds now and see where your feelings and thoughts are at. And in whatever sloppy fashion start sharing them with me.

Comment: I accept her difficulty in beginning as a real thing in itself, not just as something to be gotten out of the way so that we can deal with other issues. I also comment on it, though in ways that could easily relate to other things in her life—other times of feeling the need to be "very well organized" and be "a really good girl." My tone seems to be a sort of "teasing" one, but she apparently can sense the seriousness and helping intent in it. Despite the fact that I sometimes think of myself as mainly "client-centered" in theory, my invitation to her to share her current feelings and thoughts in "whatever sloppy fashion" seems to resemble a psychoanalytic invitation to free-associate.

C: [*laughter*] O.K., um I feel like, right now I feel as far as all things that are happening about my life right now, I, I'm really, I have a strange feeling about it, but I really can't pinpoint what it is. It's like this whole action and reaction thing between Dick and I as far as the separation—it's like, it's like very changeable. It's been changing like every day it changes drastically, and it's like I really don't know where I stand, like I'm still having feelings about am I doing the right thing, am am I being honest with myself and with Dick. Am I, um, am I doing the best that I can right now?

T: It would be so damn nice to be able to be certain.

C: I know that I can't be certain. I know that only time will tell.

T: Sure, but the longing is really there, isn't it?

C: Yes, that's something that I have, like that goes into a lot of different aspects of my life, I want to know, you know? And I know that I can't, but I feel like I have to, so I can plan for it, and that makes me really anxious.

T: And if I'm hearing you right, if you're not certain, then you might make mistakes.

C: Right, well the thing about it is not so much, it's like I'm not really afraid of making an honest mistake; it's just that when I go through all these things, like the changes that I'm trying to make in my life right now, I feel like, like we went into this a little bit. Um, I feel one way, and then I feel another way because I start thinking paranoid thoughts about what other people are thinking, like I'm not doing right, and then I think maybe I'm not doing right, and then I get to the point where I don't even know what I really think. And a lot of the time those things get confused and I don't know if I'm really doing the thing that I honestly believe in because it gets, all this other stuff gets so muddled that it's hard for me to really know exactly what I'm thinking and what I want. What I want, not what I think people think I'm doing. Sometimes it's, it's really hard to separate those: for me to think the things that I think other people are thinking, and to think the things that I am thinking. Because, they just go around in circles sometimes to the point where I don't even know what I think.

T: Kind of like the boundaries get blurred, and it's hard to say where do I stop and somebody else begins?

Comment: I try to reflect her fear of making mistakes, but I also try to make clear that this "fear" is *my* impression of what is happening and may not fit just where she is at. I have the sense that I have, in fact, missed something about the world of feeling in which she now finds herself. As I listen further in the part given above, I remember things I have read about the blurring of boundaries between "self" and "not-self" which sometimes occurs in so-called schizophrenic persons. I check out to see if that is part of where she is at, *not* because I think she is schizophrenic but because it begins to fit my sense of her at the moment.

C: Right, and that I don't like that feeling, because I, I don't feel like I have control over what I'm doing. I, I feel like I have some control, because in the end I will decide, but I feel like I don't have all of the control that I could possibly have by just being able to just be me and not try to be things or act like things that I think that I should be. And it just gets really really confusing sometimes. It just, I don't know, it gets me, if it goes like that for any more than two or three days, I just, I just get really depressed and I can't think about anything. Like I had a day like that yesterday. I was just—I woke up and it was a rotten morning and I just was really depressed all day, and I couldn't think about anything. It was like I'd try to think about something and, and my head wouldn't work, cuz I was really down and I hate it when I get down like that because if frightens me and I can't see any good, and whenever I feel depressed I always feel like I'm not gonna come out of it. I feel like—I feel like everything, nothing is worth my time to put into it, 'cause I'm just gonna die anyway. And going into um, kind of going into the thing of wanting to know exactly what's gonna happen which is absolutely impossible. Like going into my—I guess, I guess I can call my beliefs about life and an afterlife and whatever. It's like those are all muddled. Like I really don't, I don't believe in anything and I believe in everything, is what it kind of boils down to, and that makes me really nervous a lot of the time. Just, like I feel like I'm under pressure to decide what I believe in right now. Otherwise something horrible is gonna happen, but I don't really know what it is. It's just I feel like I'm gonna be wrong and it's gonna be my fault that I was wrong.

T: And I guess I just keep hearing over and over again that it's just terrible to be wrong.

C: I–I–I feel, I feel that way. I feel like I should be right. Like I know that I can't be right all the time, but I feel like I should be right for myself all the time. And a lot of times I can't decipher all these things that are happening and I don't know what's right for me. Like I just feel if I can do what's right for me that I will be happier. But a lot of times—like I don't know what it is, you know—because these boundaries have been so blurred for so long that it's really hard. Like this is the first time that I've ever really thought about myself as far as telling Dick that I want a separation. You know, it's the first time that I've actually thought about myself in terms of my happiness and long range, you know and my happiness and I, I really feel guilty about it. I can't get over that feeling of feeling guilty.

T: O.K., let's see if I catch that, though, Jane. If I hear you; this time you've managed the boundary problem. You've figured out it was really you who wanted a separation and this time you did do something that you know came from you. And shit, you still felt lousy!

C: Right, yeah, I feel really guilty about it, because I feel like I, I feel like I shouldn't think about myself first, but I know that I have to if I want to be happy, cuz nobody else is going to, especially somebody like Dick, because he's a very selfish person.

T: I guess maybe I hear something else for you, and you can tell me if this seems to fit. I hear that if you don't think about yourself pretty clearly and definitely you're just in a mess about everything and with everybody.

C: Right, I feel that way because I just, I feel like there's something that I have to figure out and understand before I can go outside of these boundaries. Like I feel, I feel like I have to know where I'm coming from before I know where I'm going. I guess it can kind of boil down to that a little bit. Um, I just, I get, when I get, when I have to think about too many things at one time, and I know that a lot of things that I think about are just, they're just created in my head—problems and pressures and stuff. They're just in my head, they're not really there. Well for me they're really there, you know?

T: Yeah.

C: And um, I feel like I shouldn't, I feel like I shouldn't, I don't have to be that way. You know, I feel like I don't have to. I can just, if I could just—all the time I'm trying to organize everything and trying to sort everything out and like I can't do it, because there's just too many things, you know. There's just no way that I can do it.

T: Let me see. Are you telling me in part that you not only feel that you've got to be right and got to understand where you're at, you have to understand everything about it right away?

Comment: She makes the powerful comment that nothing seems worthwhile, " 'cause I'm just gonna die anyway." Yet I do not respond to this. I think it is because she is still going full steam ahead, and I do not want to get into the way of her own exploration of where she is at. By the time it feels right to make a comment, I am struck with her terror of being wrong. Perhaps that is less powerful than the death theme, but I choose it because it seems to me to be the feeling she is having at that very moment. I am close, though not quite on, and my hanging in close brings us to her feelings of guilt. As I listen further, I feel that in trying to enter into her fear of mistakes and of losing a sense of self, I have underestimated the extreme urgency of her search. I try to share now my sense of that urgency.

C: Right, and it's like I feel like I have to file them in certain, um, categories. You know, like what. It's like I can't think of myself as a whole person. It's like I think of myself as a mother, and I think of myself as a wife, and I think of myself as me, and I think of myself as the neighbors down the street from some other people. It's like I'm always looking at myself through what I think the other people are looking at me, through their eyes. And like I really can't do that, cuz it's all a function to begin with on my part. Like I don't know what anybody else is thinking and I just, I feel like I have to sort all this out so I can have everything clear to me and like I know that I can't do it. I know that I can't sort out all of those things. It's impossible to do for anybody. I think.

T: O.K., let's try something for an experiment, I don't know if it'll work, but let's just take one of those roles and let's take the current one. Jane as a patient in therapy here.

C: O.K.

T: Tell me about her.

Comment: I want to deal with the here-and-now. The here-and-now, the present moment, includes her memories but it also includes this moment of relationship between the two of us. I have to overcome any false modesty and accept that how she sees me and us now is important to her. I take this moment to explore how she sees the role of client, perhaps partly to indicate that it is a role that I regard with respect. We need to know how we may see it differently. One of my supervisors from my student days, a highly psychoanalytically trained woman, probably helped me to learn this sort of thing by constantly saying, "Explore the transference." Well, "transference" notions may be one valid way of conceiving of what we next explore together, but it is not the only way.

C: Tell me . . . O.K., she's somebody who gets really upset when I'm late. Somebody who feels like I have to act a certain way in order to benefit ah, most effectively from what's happening here. Um, I feel, I feel like I have to play the role of client.

T: Tell me more about that role. I want to know what clients have to do in your world.

C: I just feel like I have to be totally honest and, um, even though sometimes I might not want to be, um, I have to talk about anything on my mind even if I feel I don't want to talk about it. Um, I feel like, I feel like you're expecting me to react in certain ways to certain things that you say. Um . . .

T: Tell me about some of the things I expect of you as you see it?

C: Um, I just, I–I feel like, well, I feel like, I feel like there's just a certain role that a client is, plays, when they come in here. Like I know that's not true, but that's what I feel inside of me. Um, other things that I expect from you?

T: Yeah, well, you know, I'd like to know more of the dimensions of that role. I hear you saying that you've gotta be honest.

C: Um, I feel like, I feel like, let's see, how can I put this into words? Sometimes I feel like I'm not an individual when I come in here, because I feel that you are gonna look at me and say oh, you know, I read that in a textbook one time. Sometimes I feel like I'm gonna be a textbook case.

T: I recognize you from page three hundred forty-five.

C: O.K., um, I feel like there are certain—Which book? [*laughs*] I feel like there are certain . . .

T: The red one! Five over on the left.

Comment: Our joking here certainly doesn't sound very psychoanalytic. It comes for me out of my sense of the flow of the relationship. It could, in the abstract, be ruled that such "teasing" is inappropriate. But, in fact, she seems to take it as I mean it: not as a put-down but as paying respect to the fact that she has the strength to humanly joke about her genuine struggles. It may catch her off guard; it is not the therapy style she is used to from before. But she accepts it and moves forward.

C: O.K.! I feel like, there's something I want to say and I can't quite get it out. I feel like there are certain certain ways that you would use to ah get me to react to certain things. And I feel like if I could pick up on thinking that you were trying to make me react a certain way then I would feel like I would have to react the way that you expected me to react and not the way that I would just react without even thinking about anything. I think about that, sometimes.

T: O.K., let me see. There are two parts to that if I'm following. One is the assumption that I have a certain set of rules or expectations. And the other part is, as you catch on to each of them, you're afraid that you're going to meet them whether that's true about you or not.

C: Right, I feel that way sometimes. Like I, like I really don't know that much about the techniques. And ah it's like, I don't know, like sometimes when I feel like you're using a certain technique, I feel like I'm being baited sometimes.

T: Do you have any examples?

C: Um, one where you might say something to me where you would want me to get mad at you, say like as an authoritarian figure to me [*laughter*] um, this is just an example. Um, you know and maybe I wouldn't; maybe I'd just say well, fuck you, you know and I—

T: You wouldn't get mad at me, you'd just say "Fuck you!"

C: Well, I mean, yeah that sounded kinda stupid, um . . .

T: But it stands as an example of how you do get trapped, doesn't it? That somehow in that example you ended up getting sucked back into meeting somebody's expectations again. And I do hear that that is what you're afraid of. I do hear you saying, "Wow, how do I find out where the real me is?"

C: Right! It's like I'm searching through all this stuff, you know, through all the ways that I think and the ways that I feel about things and there's only been a really very few occasions in my life when I really felt like me and not like the me that I think that I should be or the me that I think that I have to be. Um. . . .

T: I wonder if you have any thoughts or fantasies about what I could do here that would help you more freely be you?

C: Mmm . . . I, I really don't know, like you, I really can't think of anything really. Like, I like the way that you talk back with me a lot more, like that does um ease a lot of tensions for me. When I am, when I, oh, with Mr. Stevens, a lot of times I felt that, a lot of times like I'd ask him something, and he'd say "I can't say that." And I used to get really mad, you know? 'Cause I'd think, God, you know, why can't we just talk? You know? And um, I felt like then that I was blowing his technique by doing that, but um, I don't know, like I really can't think of anything that you could do that would make me feel more comfortable. I don't know, you radiate being relaxed and, um, you give me, you know, you talk back and forth with me and I like that.

T: O.K., and I'm glad that you see me as giving good stuff in that way, cuz I want to, but let me invite you, that when you're suspicious of what I'm doing, that when you feel pushed around, complain.

C: O.K.

T: It may be that sometimes I might do that without realizing it. And if you complain and it doesn't seem to me to fit right away, I'm willing to stop a minute and take a look at it with you. Just as I'll ask you to look at things if you know we disagree in the other direction.

Comment: I am glad she senses that I am really trying to be there with her. Perhaps my willingness to be open, compared to her previous therapist, does leave her feeling freer and less open to secret manipulation. I am trying to honestly own both my good intent and my fallibility. She is to remain the final expert on whatever I suggest about where she may be. I want her to know that we are striving for a dialogue in which we will respect each other, without asking for perfection.

C: O.K., um, getting back into that, um, feeling like I'm baited, a lot of times I feel like that. Um, I never used to until I started to know people a little bit better. You know like when I realize that people use me for certain things. Um, I have no feeling that you would use me in here for anything, but it just made me think about when I first got married, Dick used to bait me all the time. He'd ask me questions just to see if I knew, you know. And like I'd think you know, he's just asking me because he wants to know or he wants to talk about something. And I'd say, "Well, I don't know," and he'd rattle off some long detailed answer of the question that he's just asked me. It used to make me feel all the time, my God, you know! It made me feel really, it made me feel really inferior. It made me feel like he was just using me. He was just trying to see how much I knew without coming out and asking. I mean . . .

T: O.K., I'm not sure that I get your main hunch on that. Is it mainly that he wanted to know more about you, or that he wanted you to feel dumb?

C: I think that . . . I don't think it was so much that he wanted me to feel dumb, but I think that he just wanted to feel smarter. But in the process of that I did feel, you know, I felt really inferior to him. And I used to ask him about it, and I used to ask him about it and he goes "I don't know what you're talking about." Then I'd give him, you know, examples when it had happened you know, like the day before or the week before, and I go "please don't do that." You know, that really makes me feel inferior. It makes me feel like, it makes me feel like a real dummy, cuz he's a stickler for details, you know, and I'm not. And when he used to do that to me all the time, like I started thinking that other people were doing that too and I felt I've really lost all my self-confidence, cuz he used to do things like that to me all the time, and like I realize now I should have just, you know, known what I knew in my own head and not let him decide what I was gonna feel and what I did.

T: And so it started with Dick and then it spread to your feeling that a lot of people kind of use you to make themselves feel better, and you got lost in the shuffle.

Comment: At first, I'm uncertain as to why her husband played his questioning "game" with her. When I admit my uncertainty, she puts me on the right track. I can then follow and share more accurately in her feeling. I see, too, how it generalizes to her interactions with others.

C: Right, I feel that way a lot of times and it's like, when I'm around, when I'm around people that, um, I'm friends with and are not really that highly educated or, um, are not really into the intellectual segment of our society, I feel like I'm really together and and like that I'm not really dumb, like a lot of times I think I am. I feel like I am, I know that I'm not, but I feel like I am sometimes. And when I get in with people—oh, for an example, we have a friend of ours who's a doctor and we were over his house one day and he had some friend of his over there from Holland. And he, he was like this super-physicist. He was so overtrained that he couldn't get a job. He was over here looking for a job, and like when I get around people like that I just think, oh God, you know, they can't possibly want to know anything I have to say. You know, they can't, they can't possibly have any interest in anything that I would say. I feel like I couldn't even shine their shoes when it comes to having a conversation. And as it turned out, the guy was really nice. We sat and yacked all night, but I still had, I still had this feeling inside of me that I wasn't, I wasn't as good or I wasn't . . .

T: O.K., so I guess I hear another part of it. You suspected that you'd have nothing to say to this guy and he'd have nothing to say to you and that made you feel really low, and dumb and inferior. And then when it turned out you were wrong, you stayed feeling low and dumb and inferior.

C: Um, yeah, because then, this is really gonna sound stupid, but you know I just . . . After I left there, I just felt like, well, they were just being nice. And like I *know* that they weren't, you know, I mean they were really, they were honest people.

T: But boy, it's so hard to really feel and believe that you're any good.

C: It is for me, a lot of times and like I have lots of reasons to not think that way and not feel that way and it's like constantly, it's it's like if I don't get assurance all the time then I feel like I'm no good. And what I want to do is, I want to get away from relying on that. Like, it's nice when I get a compliment or something, or somebody says something that is good about me to me. I feel really good, but I don't want to be dependent on that to feel good. And like most of the time right now I am and I . . . It's not good because it works the other way too, you know. It's like when I don't get the reassurance then I feel just rotten.

T: And it's really a two-way thing, and I really hear that. Let me kind of tell you in terms of my value system what I would like for you. And you know, you don't have to agree. What I would really like for you is for you to decide that you're not rateable. Because, if I can get you to believe you're rated good, then somebody could still rate you bad— whereas I'd like you to be unrateable.

Comment: I first got this notion of the importance of being *un*ratable from Albert Ellis. Although much of Ellis's Rational–Emotive therapy is quite different from my approach, I am glad to have gotten this powerful concept from it. I am sharing with my client here that this is a value of my own. I mean to be honestly myself here without forcing my values on her.

C: Right! It's like I, I understand that you know, like I, like I know that I can't, I can't rate myself against anybody because what am I gonna rate against, you know? Like we're all, we're all into different things. But I just always have that feeling, especially when I get around new people. Unless, unless I can see that they're really out of tune as far as I'm concerned—then I don't feel, I don't feel inferior. And then again, like that's—just my own opinion of them, you know, like, it's like I, it's like I can't get away from feeling that I always have to judge and be judged and, and I don't like doing it, 'cause I—don't feel it's right. I don't, I don't feel that I can gain anything by it. I, I feel like I only have things to lose by doing that, and I can't seem to break away from that. And I, I'm trying, you know like, I'm trying to concentrate on doing things just the way I want to do them and not even thinking about anybody else. And I've started to do it a little bit.

T: It comes to my mind as you're talking. I find myself thinking kind of as if there's some really bad stuff about you and anybody who listens to you too closely or too carefully is going to find out those horrible things, and then they'll know where to rate Jane.

C: Um, I think, I think part of it's, it kind of goes along those lines. It's like a lot of times I think, well for example, the kids. You know like sometimes I just, sometimes I just don't want any kids around me at all, and they're around me all the time. Like, I went out yesterday and I got a job, so, a part-time job because it's something that I've been wanting to do to get a little bit of extra money and to, um, get away from the kids cuz they drive me nuts when I'm around 'em all the time. And I feel really rotten, I feel like a rotten mother when I look at those kids and go, "I don't want you anywhere near me, goddamnit." You know, "Leave me alone." And I feel like that is just the most rotten thing I can do. 'Cause those kids, you know, they're just being kids. They, you know, like, they, you know, it's just me not coping with them. It's not them. It's just me on those days when they get on my nerves or I've had too much kids. And that makes me feel really rotten. And, and perspective-wise, like when I look around . . .

T: Um, there's something I should tell you, Jane. I've already decided you're imperfect.

Comment: I remember hearing from Ellis his syllogism: "Human beings are imperfect; you are a human being, therefore you are imperfect!" Ellis's style in therapy—such as the examples you can hear on AAP Tape No. C-34—is often a harsher, more confrontative one than mine. I think that the Ellis influence is really getting to me in the next few minutes of this therapy session. The client takes it pretty well, but my confronting "jokes" here do not seem to me quite fully my own style.

C: O.K., I know. I know that.

T: I put it in my notes the first day.

C: [*laughter*] It's just, it's like, when it comes to something like that, like I really, with that particular thing with the kids, it's like I really don't think about what other people think. I think about, I think about the kids and I think that I, that I'm really gonna fuck 'em up if I do that. That's another thing I, well like with Richie you know it's not too bad. But with [*her daughter*], the first one, man! Every single thing that I did, I felt like it was gonna make such a deep dent on her brain. That she was gonna remember every single thing that happened.

T: She's how old?

C: She's almost three.

T: She's psychotic already?

C: No, she's not.

T: After all those bad things you did?

C: I really didn't do all those bad things, you know, but to me I feel like they're horrible.

T: The data doesn't look that way, does it?

C: Pardon me?

T: The data doesn't look that way.

C: No, no, it doesn't. Like I, like I know that I'm, I know that I'm a good mother, you know? It's just that, I don't know, I think a lot about it. I know a lot of it goes back to what I, what my mother did and in, and how she raised us.

T: Somewhere along the line from your mother, from wherever, from your own conclusions, you really learned well that you are a shit.

C: Yeah, I feel that way a lot of times. Like, well like now at least, sometimes I can feel like I might be doing something a little bit worthwhile.

T: Considering.

C: [*laughter*] Yes, but you know, like for, it's like I can't like myself.

T: Even when you tell me you did something worthwhile, I really hear you saying, "Isn't that worthwhile for a shitty lady to have done?"

C: Yeah, I feel that about myself and it's like I can't, it's like I can't overcome that feeling inside of me that I am no good. And there is nothing, there is nothing that I could do that would be good that could ever make up for how bad I am. And I try, I try to understand,

I try to think back, I try to think to what point, you know, how did I, when did I start thinking about myself like that? And it goes all the way back.

T: Yes. Before even trying to travel back there with you, Jane, I guess I want to tell you that, wow, that sounds like a terrible feeling to live with.

Comment: I feel her pain so sharply that I want to tell her my sense of it right away. If she then wants to move to the past to search for its origins, that's all right with me. She doesn't, however. She stays in the actions and feelings of the current stretch of her life. I think my understanding and acceptance of the "terrible feeling" she is living with makes it easier for her to stay in the present. She can speak about it directly without using the past as a distancing metaphor for what she is feeling right now.

C: Yeah, it is, it really gets me down sometimes. I guess that I felt, why the fuck should I do anything? I, you know, like anything that I do doesn't mean shit. Any, anything, anything that I do is, is, is, it's nothing. Anybody could'a done it.

T: How could it be worthwhile if I did it?

C: Yeah, I feel that way a lot of times and it really makes me mad. It makes me mad and it makes me depressed and it makes me, it makes me well, especially depressed a lot of times. And, it's like, it's like I want to overcome it so bad and, and I can't right now. I, like, I hope that I will be able to in the future, but I can't right now, for some reason. And I just, I can't stop getting all the ideas of roles out of my head. It's like, um, like with this separation thing, I feel like it's all my fault. I know it's not all my fault. I know it's nobody's fault. It's just something that happened, but I feel like it's all my fault, I feel like I'm running out on Dick. I'm rotten because I don't want to have sex with him. I'm rotten cause I don't want him to touch me. I'm rotten because I don't want him to live in my house. And he keeps on saying things to me, you know. "It's gonna be so much harder on me than it is on you 'cause you're in familiar surroundings." And that really makes me mad when he says that, 'cause I know it's not gonna be easy during the winter time and . . . But I still feel really rotten. I feel like I've caused all this unhappiness, and I just dread the day that my parents find out. Not so much my dad, but my mom, I just dread the day that my mother finds out that we're getting a separation. I just dread that day 'cause I just, she's just gonna bombard me with—how rotten Dick is, and "I knew he was never any good for you, and bla bla bla bla bla bla bla." And I don't want to hear that, you know? But ah, that's getting off onto something else though.

T: I guess I hear that you feel that your mother won't even give you the right to recognize your own mistakes and do something about them.

C: Right, it's like, it's like I've fairly understood that my mother will never understand me. I, you know, like, like I know that, but it's still sometimes you really want her to. And, like I know that she never will and I just, like when she'll say, I know that she's gonna say all that stuff about Dick. I know it, and it's gonna make me feel here I am writing out the script, but I have a feeling it's gonna, she's gonna infer that I, I didn't, I wasn't good enough to know all these things. You know, like I wasn't smart enough, like anything I do she criticizes it, anything I do. You know, like I, like I'm startin' to get away from it, you know, but I really get pissed off, because I think back to when I was younger. And I think of all the times when I had really neat ideas and things that I wanted to do, and gee, "You can't do that." You know? "People will think you're nuts." Um. "The nuns won't like that." Um, just there was so many strict rules that I had to live by when I was a kid. It's like I don't even . . . I'm realizing every day, you know, more things that I, more strict rules that I had to live by as a kid and it makes me really mad. And at the same time I feel like I shouldn't be wasting my time thinking about that, I should be spending my time putting the energies into getting away from that.

T: Into somehow finally becoming a grown-up.

C: Right! And um like I just, I feel like, I feel like I have a compulsion though too, to look at those things for some reason just to get mad, I guess. I sometimes think I want to look at all those things to get mad so I can, so I can have an excuse for being as rotten as I am to myself.

T: O.K., well let's try that for a minute. I guess I'm responding to some of the same things. I'm not sure that we've got the reasons right, but I do have the sense that it's important to you to be angry.

Comment: The importance of her anger is becoming clearer and clearer to us both. But it is so easy in our society—so many of us have been taught this way—to try to turn away from anger and *pretend* it isn't there. My comment on her anger here may help her to stay with it and search for a fuller awareness of it. It also shows that I can accept anger, perhaps that I can even believe it may be of value.

C: Right, it's like, it's like I'm really super-resentful of the schools that I went to. I'm really resentful of all the things that my mother, um, put up with through the school and through the church that I can't believe that anybody with common sense, with any love of their kids would ever make their kids do those things. But I understand she thought it was right. I understand that. It's, it's more the church and the school that I really get pissed at.

T: What would happen if you weren't angry about it?

C. What would happen if I wasn't angry about it? If I wasn't angry about it, I probably wouldn't ever be aware of it. I mean, I'm only speaking for myself.

T: Let me try and guess. Um, the thought strikes me that maybe if you forgot to be angry, you might be afraid of becoming just unbearably sad.

Comment: Although I have many reservations about standard psychoanalytic ways of doing therapy, I often find the psychoanalytic way of understanding persons to be of much value. I am aware here of the analytic notion that depression or great sadness may be a result of anger turned against the self. And I am thinking of the corollary: that anger may save one from such sadness.

C: Mmmm, I, I've thought about that at one, a couple of times. Like, I've . . . I was really sad that those things happened to me, all those things that I think were just really horrible and I figured there was nothing I could do about it, you know? So I, I figured, you know, I can't go back. You know, there's nothing that I can do about what already happened and that I should try. Well, at the time, at the time when it did happen, when I was looking at those things, I did feel sad that I had to go through them and felt sorry for myself about having to do all those things when I was a kid and lived under very rigid restrictions. At the time, my sister-in-law whose life was just, oh, God, her childhood was just one of the worst I've ever heard of. She was going through a thing and I, I just felt like I had . . . With the problems that she had, mine were nothing compared to the, to the obstacles that she had to overcome in her childhood 'cause I didn't have it as bad as she did. I mean she had it from everywhere including her family. And I, everything, everything, she was rejected everywhere she went and I think to myself at least I was accepted some places. Like I really feel like there weren't that many places where I really was truly accepted as myself, but, um, I just kind of put it out of my mind, you know, of being sad, you know, 'cause I just, I felt sorrier for Laurie than I did for myself at that point. And I, in the meantime, I've not, never really felt really sad about it, I've just felt very resentful and very angry. I mean so angry sometimes that I just felt like going over and bombing the place so they couldn't fuck up any more kids.

T: Just really enraged.

C: Right, and it, it, and it just it makes me really mad, because all these other thousands of kids that get get that everyday—you know, goin' to those schools. I'm, I'm sure you know, like for some of 'em it's probably all right 'cause maybe when they grow up they'll believe in it, you know. But, I just never could get into what they were trying to do. And what they were trying to teach me as far as religion and life goes. I never could really get into it. You know, I just, I just always thought that it was stupid. And when I'd voice that, then I was rotten and I was nuts 'cause I didn't believe it and I was possessed with the devil and bla bla bla bla bla bla . . . You know, so the . . .

T: So they were only part-way successful. They didn't teach you to believe in those things. They only taught you to believe you're bad and stupid.

Comment: I am trying to follow her story and her feelings. I share my provisional understanding of the bind she was in. She accepts it, and then I share with her the parallel I seem to see between that parochial school bind and what is happening now in her marriage.

C: Right, they taught, they taught me to believe that, um, if I didn't conform to what they thought that I should be and what I should believe in, then there was no hope for me at all. None! You know, I might as well just ah you know hang it up, and like when I think back to that it really pisses me off really bad.

T: Yeah, something like that seems to have happened in the marriage with Dick too. You got to the point where you no longer believed that you should behave in a certain way towards him. You said hey, I'm not gonna be a wife, or at least that kind of wife anymore. I know that doesn't fit, but you still believe that you're bad and stupid.

C: Right, and I, it's like, it's like: I'm feeling guilty for something that I don't believe in. And I can't figure out why. It's like I want to know why, you know, 'cause I feel, I feel like I have to know why so I can overcome it, you know. And I can't understand why. You know I just, I just can't, I can't answer that to myself and I know that it's not just one, one simple sentence that's gonna solve everything. I know it's a lot of things but I, I don't know what those things are and it just, I don't know, it just really makes me feel hopeless sometimes 'cause I feel . . . I feel that I'll never know what they are, and I feel like I can't help myself to overcome these things unless I know what I have to overcome and then I start thinking, well maybe that's an excuse cuz you really don't have to know what the things are to overcome 'em [*laughter*]. Then I start feeling like I'm spending too much time thinking about things that have happened, instead of trying to just, um, do the best right now and, and kind of make a clean slate type of thing.

T: Jane, I don't want to be insensitive to the kind of pain and distress you're talking about, but I guess I want to know another side of you too . . . Can you tell me some good things about you?

Comment: In reading this, my switch of topic here seems surprising to me. Listening to it on tape, the sounds of our voices make it seem less abrupt and disruptive. She seems to have, in a sense, finished a piece of work. She has found in herself an over-attachment to past pain, and she has identified it clearly for both of us. But I am strongly aware that this story of pain—past and present— is not her whole story. I am trying to express my interest in all of who she is: the parts she values as well as those she condemns.

C: Yeah, I'm, I'm um I'm pretty friendly. I, I help my friends out whenever I can. And if there's any way that they need help and I can help 'em, well I'll help 'em. Um, I don't waste things. Um, I'm really a hard worker. I work harder than I should sometimes.

T: Oh, you did it again!!

Comment: She has obviously just gone back to picking on herself. It felt to me that to reflect this too somberly would be to return to the tone of a catalogue of woes and flaws. My "mocking" is meant—and, I believe, accepted—as a respect to her strength. We do continue more seriously after that.

C: [*laughter*] I work hard. Let me put it this way. Let me put it this way. I work harder than I have to a lot of times. That, that's not . . .

T: I heard ya.

C: I work harder than what I can get by with.

T: O.K.

C: Um, um I'm . . .

T: But you can't talk for very long without getting down on you.

C: Yeah, I, it's like I want to look at the good things cuz I know there's a lot of good things. And, and it's like I just, I think way back in the back of my mind somewhere I feel like I have to be perfect, otherwise I'm not worthwhile [*laughter*]. And, and that's silly—but sometimes I think, sometimes I think that.

T: But you really are a perfectionist, aren't you?

C: Um, yeah in a lot of ways, I–I feel like if I can't do it right then I'm not even gonna do it. You know, I feel if I, if I'm only gonna do it half-heartedly then why even bother to do it, even though there are things that I do half-heartedly, cuz I have to do them, but as far as things, you know, my own set of things that I want to do myself . . . .

T: I will not be another of the world's half-asses.

C: Right.

T: I will be either perfectly successful—

C: —or perfectly unsuccessful, and God! I've never thought of that before. It's, it's hard for me to travel the middle road [*laughter*]. And that's I guess that's exactly what we're talking about.

T: And therefore, since you're human and humans are imperfect, if you can't be perfect you're gonna be a total utter failure.

C: Right, I feel that a lot of times. Um, like I don't know why, you know?

T: But, you told me why . . .

C: What?

T: You told me that it's better to be an utter shit than to be half-assed.

Comment: This is a good example of how material from a wide variety of sources may occur to me during therapy. The idea that she must be either perfectly successful or perfectly unsuccessful, that she must not be "half-assed," occurred to me at the moment because of a poem I had learned years before which suddenly popped into my head:

THE ATLAS

by Heinrich Heine

I, a wretched Atlas,
a world,
the whole world of pain,
I must carry.

I bear the unbearable,
and my heart pushes to tear and burst.

You, stubborn heart,
you wanted it just so.
You wanted happiness unending,
or else unending suffering.

Proud, stubborn heart,
And now, you suffer.

Translated by Ezra Ben Shimon

C: Well. Yeah, yeah I, it's, it's that people that are half-assed really really
bug the shit out of me and I don't want to be like that. [*laughter*] And
it's, it's like I keep thinking to myself if I could know exactly what I
want, then, um, then I can put all my energies into—
T: And you can only know exactly what you want.
C: Right. I want to know exactly what I want, you know? I really want to
know exactly what I want. That's the only way I can put it.
T: If I could know exactly what I want and do it perfectly, then I'd be
happy and till then I'm on strike.
C: [*laughter*] I, it's, that's kinda like . . . That's kinda like putting into
words a feeling that I've had a lot of times that I've been unable to
put into words. Um, a feeling I want to do something, but something's in my way and I don't know what it is. I've had that feeling so
many times and and before I used to think it was some outside thing.
Now I know it's just me. [*laughter*] Um, there's just, there's so many
things that I want to do that I can't decide on what I want to do, and I
know that I can't do all of them all at once. I mean like, there's a lot
of things that I would like to go to school and be and I can't decide on
which one I want to be, so I, I don't know. I didn't go to school—
T: Since I may not choose the perfect right thing: Nothing!
C: Right, it's like I feel! I feel like if I do want to be trained to do
something, it's like I think, well, if I choose this, then I think, well
God, maybe I'd—after I get to know that I'll really be bored with it
and I'll really hate it. And I should look in terms of "Hey, well if it
gets to that point, I'll just go back to school and do something else, or
don't do that anymore, do something else." But in my head I feel like
that's the end. If I did that, and it didn't work out . . . If I couldn't do
this and it doesn't work out, then then I—I fucked up somewhere.
You know like it's ah, I think it's just, it's just that you know like it's
my fault that this didn't work out cuz I should'a known these things.

And I should'a gone and done the other thing that I was thinking about, but I chose this one instead.

T: I should, I should, I should. . . .

Comment: She has so many rules, so many "shoulds"! I sometimes see people—clients, therapists and others—as dragging around with massive rule books chained to their legs. Limping from that hampering weight. I am not against rules, but I do believe that many of us have too many of them and too many outdated ones. I think we need our rule books, but I think they need regular re-examination and editing.

C: Yeah, I it's like, it's like I think to myself, there's a lot of things that I could probably do and be happy doing 'em. But somewhere inside of me there is something that says there's only one thing that you can do and, and if you do other things, then if you do other things then you're not being real with yourself.

T: O.K., I hear the—

C: If I can kinda, I was just gonna say that that I, ah that really sounded confusing to me as it came out, but that's how it is in my head. It's, it's kind of confusing anyway.

T: O.K.

C: You had kind of a puzzled look on you, like what the hell is she talking about? [*langhter*]

T: No, the puzzle would be something else. I think you're reading my expression right, but I'm aware of the fact that we don't have much more time, and I remembered something that I don't know, that I wanted to ask about, so that was the puzzle.

C: [*laughter*] O.K.

Comment: Although I was not puzzled about what she was saying then, I tried to find sone part of me that she was accurately perceiving. She was, in fact, noticing a change in my expression. I was realizing that I had not picked up on some factual information about her; I had not gotten the details I needed for following her story as well as her feelings. I did that now.

T: Ah, I have a sense that besides this stuff which is certainly important, I also want some more information about where you are in time and in space, and I want to know what your part-time job is?

C: [*laughter*] I'm going to be working in Rose's Delicatessen [*laughter*] I just, um, it's, it's gonna be fun.

Comment: It sounds like her new job, although only a waitress position, holds some fun for her. In the atmosphere we have established with each other, it does seem to have become possible to talk about fun, as well as anguish. We talked together for a few more minutes—not captured on tape—and the therapy session ended.

APPENDIX

The Client Perception Questionnaire

Chapter 5 of this book lists the six perceptions of the therapist which I believe the client must hold for effective growth and progress in therapy to take place. Shortly after I finished the first edition of this book (where those six "perceptions" were essentially the same as here), I began working on an empirical way of measuring those six factors. I constructed a scale of 60 statements listing a variety of ways a client might see a therapist as feeling or behaving toward the client. The client is asked to rate each item on a seven point scale. There are ten items for each of the six client perceptions. For example, one of the items which scores on my Fourth Client Perception scale—having to do with empathy—is: "She tries to see things through my eyes." (I have put "She" as the pronoun in this example; obviously it would be "He" if the questionnaire were being used to describe a client's view of a male therapist. I use two "forms" of the Client Perception Questionnaire (CPQ): a male and a female form differing only in the gender of the pronouns.)

Half of the ten items for each client perception are phrased in a negative way in order to balance for response set (a tendency to always put down high numbers, for example, regardless of content). Thus, one of the items related to my first client perception—having to do with congruence—is: "I feel she is being genuine with me," while a negatively phrased one on that same perception is: "What she says gives me a false impression of her total reaction to me." Items pertaining to the various client perceptions are mixed randomly within the total 60 items of the Client Perception Questionnaire (CPQ). At the end of this Appendix is the CPQ as I use it, together with the Tally Sheet for scoring which helps to keep track of which items score on which scale.

I feel it is important first to say something about the connection between the CPQ and the Barrett-Lennard Relationship Inventory, a research instrument which has been described in earlier chapters of this book. The items of the CPQ were, in part, written by me together with some of my friends and colleagues. But close to one-quarter of the items come from the original form of the Relationship Inventory (Barrett-Lennard, 1962). The theories behind that Inventory and the CPQ resemble each other enough that the excellent wording of numerous items in that earlier Inventory made them useful for the purposes of the CPQ. The Relationship Inventory (RI) is still in extensive use. The RI is, in fact, designed to investigate a number of relationships in addition to the therapy one, while the CPQ is specifically written for the kind of client-therapist model described in Chapter 5 of this book. Those items "borrowed" from the RI appear here in the first published version of the CPQ through the kind permission of Professor Barrett-Lennard and the American Psychological Association.

Some research involving the CPQ is already completed, and more is in progress. Work on an earlier version of the CPQ, almost identical with the form given at the end of this Appendix, has helped establish the reliability of the Questionnaire (Louy, 1974). Odd-even reliabilities for different rater groups ranged from correlations of .80 to .96. Louy also found a highly significant relationship between clients' ratings of the "Helpfulness" of their therapy sessions (as measured by the Therapy Session Report of Orlinsky and Howard, 1975) and both total CPQ scores and scores on Scale IV. A study on sex of therapist and client (Blase, 1978) found that clients who have therapy with therapists of their own sex have significantly higher CPQ scores than those with opposite-sex therapists. Lipka (1978) used the CPQ in a study of group therapy with cancer patients. Among her findings (not all of which have yet been analyzed) was a very high test–retest reliability for the CPQ.

I myself use the CPQ in my therapy practice. When I have a sense that therapy is not progressing well, I ask the client to complete the CPQ. We then look together at the resulting scores, and it gives us an idea of how I may not be coming across well on one or more of the Client Perceptions which I believe are essential for therapeutic growth. I look at which of the client perception scores is lowest, and I consider the total CPQ score. *Very tentatively* (pending further use and research), I have come to think of total CPQ scores below 100 as probably indicating problems in the therapy relationship. Scores between 100 and 125 may or may not go with some problems in the therapy. Scores between 125 and 165 seem to me to suggest a good working relationship between therapist and client. I am not sure about the meaning of scores above 165. These occur rather rarely in my experience, and until further research has accumulated, I am even more hesitant to comment on those than on the ranges I have already noted.

The CPQ and the Tally Sheet follow. The CPQ is self-explanatory. The Tally Sheet indicates which items score on which scales, in addition to being a convenient way to sum up the scores. The numbers under column I of the Tally Sheet are the CPQ items which score on the first client perception: nos. 12, 15, etc. The numbers under column II are those items which score on the second client perception, and so forth. In filling in the Tally Sheet from a completed CPQ, write next to each number the scale rating score (from 0 to 6) which the client has assigned to that item. Then follow the indications on the Tally Sheet: (1) Add the scores for each column in section A, (2) add the scores for each column in section B, (3) subtract the sum of the A columns from the sum of the B columns. The bottom line then gives you the CPQ score for each of the client perceptions. The sum of those six numbers is the total CPQ score.

Further research into this approach to studying the client's experience of psychotherapy is still going on. If you write to me about it, I shall try to keep you informed about any current research, as well as trying to be helpful about any research or clinical uses of the CPQ which you are investigating. I can be reached at: The Department of Psychology, The University of Detroit, Detroit, Michigan, 48221. I am pleased to say that Grune & Stratton, Inc., the publisher of this book, grants automatic permission for use of the Client Perception Questionnaire in clinical work and research.

Client Perception Questionnaire

NAME (Or Code Number) _____

DATE _____

On these pages are listed a variety of ways that a psychotherapist might feel or behave toward a client. Please consider how true each item is as a description of how your psychotherapist is with you. If it is something that is definitely never true for him, put a zero on the line preceding the item. If it is definitely always true for him, put a six on the line. If it is somewhere in-between, put a number between zero and six to stand for how often and strongly he does show that way of feeling and behaving.

You will, then, be rating your psychotherapist for each item, on a scale from zero to six.

| definitely never true | 0 | 1 | 2 | 3 | 4 | 5 | 6 | definitely always true |

Please mark a number in for *every* item.

_____ 1. He understands how I feel.

_____ 2. He lets me see when certain things I say disturb him.

_____ 3. He tries to understand me without really considering my own point of view.

_____ 4. He understands only my words but not the way I feel.

_____ 5. He rarely insists on talking about his experience in preference to listening to mine.

definitely never true	0	1	2	3	4	5	6	definitely always true

Please mark a number in for *every* item.

_____ 6. Depending on his mood he sometimes responds to me with much less warmth and interest than he does at other times.

_____ 7. His own feelings toward some of things I say, or do, stop him from really paying attention to my needs.

_____ 8. He does not realize how strongly I feel about many of the things we discuss.

_____ 9. He respects me.

_____ 10. He feels that I am a dull and uninteresting person.

_____ 11. When I do not say very clearly what I mean, he usually fails to understand me.

_____ 12. There are times when I feel that his outward response is quite different from his inner reaction to me.

_____ 13. He never says more about himself than I really am interested in hearing.

_____ 14. He just tolerates me.

_____ 15. Sometimes he is not at all comfortable but we go on, outwardly ignoring it.

_____ 16. He sometimes is so concerned with my feelings that he misses the point of what I am trying to say.

_____ 17. He can share my disturbance when I am troubled about certain things.

_____ 18. He usually understands all of what I say to him.

_____ 19. He gives up trying to follow me when I seem to ramble.

_____ 20. He tells more about his opinions or feelings than I really want to know.

_____ 21. He does not really care what happens to me.

_____ 22. He is friendly and warm towards me.

definitely
always
true

0   1   2   3   4   5   6

Please mark a number in for *every* item.

_____ 23. He encourages me to disagree with him openly, when I feel his comments about me are wrong.

_____ 24. I feel that he is being genuine with me.

_____ 25. He never pushes his own feelings and thoughts on me when I don't want to hear them.

_____ 26. He is more interested in expressing and communicating things about himself than in knowing and understanding me.

_____ 27. I do not think that he hides anything from himself that he feels with me.

_____ 28. He is genuinely interested in me.

_____ 29. He can sometimes call my attention to facts that I didn't realize I'd even mentioned.

_____ 30. He expresses ideas or feelings of his own only when he thinks I might really be interested in them.

_____ 31. He actively tries to follow whatever I tell him.

_____ 32. He does not allow himself to become involved in my feelings.

_____ 33. He never forces me to think about him when I am concerned about other things.

_____ 34. I feel that I can trust him to be honest with me.

_____ 35. He understands what I say only from a detached objective point of view.

_____ 36. He always responds to my comments with genuine interest.

_____ 37. He gets impatient with me when I seem to move too slowly for his needs.

_____ 38. He tries to see things through my eyes.

definitely never true	0	1	2	3	4	5	6	definitely always true

Please mark a number in for *every* item.

_____ 39. His reactions show that he really knows how I feel.

_____ 40. He argues with me when we disagree and insists on the correctness of his interpretations.

_____ 41. He adopts a professional role that makes it hard for me to know what he is like as a person.

_____ 42. He pretends to understand what I am saying, even when I am sure he has missed important details.

_____ 43. He tries to feel what my experiences are like for me.

_____ 44. He disapproves of me.

_____ 45. He trusts my judgments about myself.

_____ 46. What he says gives a false impression of his total reaction to me.

_____ 47. He acts as if he were the only one capable of correctly interpreting my feelings and experiences.

_____ 48. He is willing to base much of his understanding of me on how I tell him I am feeling about myself.

_____ 49. He is most interested in knowing what my experiences mean and feel like to me.

_____ 50. He does not try to mislead me about his own thoughts and feelings.

_____ 51. He is unwilling to have me discuss my feelings further once he feels sure that he knows what they are.

_____ 52. If he doesn't understand something I say, he asks questions to clarify it.

_____ 53. He respects my opinions about myself.

_____ 54. He lets me know if I need to make facts or details clearer for him.

definitely never true	0	1	2	3	4	5	6	definitely always true

Please mark a number in for *every* item.

_____ 55. He has trouble remembering the important facts of my life even though I have told them to him.

_____ 56. Sometimes he thinks that I feel a certain way just because he feels that way.

_____ 57. He is interested in knowing about my experiences, but not in sensing what they really mean to me.

_____ 58. He is curious about the "way I tick," but not really interested in me as a person.

_____ 59. I don't think that he is being honest with himself about the way he feels towards me.

_____ 60. He cares about me.

CPQ Tally Sheet

Code Number _____ Date _____

	I	II	III	IV	V	VI
A	12	6	11	4	10	3
	15	7	16	8	14	40
	41	20	19	32	21	47
	46	26	42	35	44	51
	59	37	55	57	58	56

SUM OF A

	I	II	III	IV	V	VI
B	2	5	18	1	9	23
	24	13	29	17	22	45
	27	25	31	38	28	48
	34	30	52	39	36	49
	50	33	54	43	60	53

SUM OF B					
LESS SUM OF A					
SCALE TOTALS					

SCALE TOTALS: I   _____

                       II   _____

                     III   _____

                     IV   _____

                      V   _____

                     VI   _____

TOTAL CPQ SCORE: _____

REFERENCES

American Psychiatric Association. *Diagnostic and statistical manual, H.* Washington, D.C.: American Psychiatric Association, 1968.

Andrews, J. D. W. Psychotherapy of phobias. *Psychological Bulletin,* 1966, *66,* 455–480.

Arthur, R. J., & Gunderson, E. K. E. Stability in psychiatric diagnoses from hospital admission to discharge. *Journal of Clinical Psychology,* 1966, *22,* 140–144.

Bandura, A., & Walters, R. H. *Social learning and personality development.* New York: Holt, Rinehart and Winston, 1963.

Barrett-Lennard, G. T. Dimensions of therapist response as causal factors in therapeutic change. *Psychological Monographs,* 1962, *76* (43, Whole No. 567).

Beier, E. G. *The silent language of psychotherapy.* Chicago: Aldine, 1966.

Betz, B. J. Studies of the therapist's role in the treatment of the schizophrenic patient. *American Journal of Psychiatry,* 1967, pp. 123; 963; 971.

Blase, J. J. Client perceptions of same-sexed and opposite-sexed therapists. Presented at American Psychological Association Meetings, Toronto, 1978.

Board, F. A. Patients' and physicians' judgments of outcome of psychotherapy in an outpatient clinic. *A.M.A. Archives of General Psychiatry,* 1959, *1,* 185–196.

Breger, L., & McGaugh, J. L. Critique and reformulation of "learning theory" approaches to psychotherapy. *Psychological Bulletin*, 1965, *63*, 338–358.

Bugenthal, J. F. T. *The search for authenticity: An existential-analytic approach to psychotherapy.* New York: Holt, Rinehart and Winston, 1966.

Cameron, D. E. A theory of diagnosis. In P. H. Hoch & J. Zubin (Eds.), *Current problems in psychiatric diagnosis.* New York: Grune & Stratton, 1953.

Colby, K. M. *A primer for psychotherapists.* New York: Ronald, 1951.

Dollard, J., & Miller, N. *Personality and psychotherapy.* New York: McGraw-Hill, 1950.

Eysenck, H. J., & Rachman, S. *The causes and cures of neurosis.* San Diego: Knapp, 1965.

Feifel, H., & Eells, J. Patients and therapists assess the same psychotherapy. *Journal of Consulting Psychology*, 1963, *27*, 310–318.

Freud, S. Further recommendations in the technique of psychoanalysis: observations on transference-love. In *Collected papers* (Vol. H). London: Hogarth, 1956. (Original pub., 1915)

Freud, S. *The ego and the id.* London: Hogarth, 1927.

Freud, S. *An autobiographical study.* London: Hogarth, 1935.

Gendlin, E. T. A theory of personality change. In F. Worchel & D. Byrne (Eds.), *Personality change.* New York: Wiley, 1964.

Gendlin, E. T. Therapeutic procedures in dealing with schizophrenics. In C. R. Rogers (Ed.), *The therapeutic relationship and its impact: A study of psychotherapy with schizophrenics.* Madison: Univ. of Wisconsin, 1967.

Gendlin, E. T., Beebe, J., Cassens, J., Klein, M., & Oberlander, M. Focusing ability in psychotherapy, personality, and creativity. In J. M. Shlien (Ed.), *Research in psychotherapy* (Vol. III). Washington, D.C.: American Psychological Association, 1968.

Green, H. *I never promised you a rose garden.* New York: Signet, 1965.

Grossberg, J. M. Successful behavior therapy in a case of speech phobia. *Journal of Speech and Hearing Disorders*, 1965, *30*, 285–288.

Hoch, P. H., & Zubin, J. (Eds.). *Current problems in psychiatric diagnosis.* New York: Grune & Stratton, 1953.

Holland, G. A. *Fundamentals of psychotherapy.* New York: Holt, Rinehart and Winston, 1965.

Jourard, S. M. *The transparent self.* Princeton: Van Nostrand, 1964.

Jourard, S. M. *Disclosing man to himself.* Princeton: Van Nostrand, 1968.

Karon, B. P., & O'Grady, P. Intellectual test changes in schizophrenic patients in the first six months of treatment. *Psychotherapy: Theory, Research and Practice*, 1969, *6*, 88–96.

Kramer, E. Judgment of personal characteristics and emotions from nonverbal properties of speech. *Psychological Bulletin*, 1963, *60*, 408–420.

Kramer, E. Elimination of verbal cues in judgment of emotion from voice. *Journal of Abnormal Psychology*, 1964, *58*, 390–396.

Kreitman, N. The reliability of psychiatric diagnosis. *Journal of Mental Science*, 1961, *107*, 876–886.

Kreitman, N., Sainsbury, P., Morrissey, J., Towers, J., & Scrivner, J. The reliability of psychiatric assessment: An analysis. *Journal of Mental Science*, 1961, *107*, 887–908.

Lazarus, A. A. *Behavior therapy and beyond.* New York: McGraw-Hill, 1971.

Lazarus, A. A. Has behavior therapy outlived its usefulness? *American Psychologist*, ·1, 1977, *32*, 550–556.

Lipka, D. Rogerian conditions in group therapy with mastectomy patients. Presented at American Psychological Association meetings, Toronto, 1978.

Lorr, M., Klett, C. J., & McNair, D. M. *Syndromes of psychosis.* New York: Pergamon, 1963.

Louy, J. *The relationships between therapist's and patient's perceptions of one another during their therapy encounters and the perceptions of observing patients and therapists.* Unpublished doctoral dissertation, Adelphi University, 1973.

Mahrer, A. R. (Ed.). *The goals of psychotherapy.* New York: Appleton-Century-Crofts, Division of Meredith Publishing Company, 1967.

Maslow, A. H. *Toward a psychology of being.* Princeton: Van Nostrand, 1962.

Mills, D. H., & Zytowski, D. G. Helping relationship: A structural analysis. *Journal of Counseling Psychology*, 1967, *14*, 193–197.

Nijinsky, R. (Ed.). *The diary of Vaslav Nijinsky.* Berkeley: Univ. of Calif. Press, 1968.

Orlinsky, D., & Howard, K. *Varieties of psychotherapeutic experience.* New York: Teachers College Press, 1975.

Powell, W. J. Differential effectiveness of interviewer interventions in an experimental setting. *Journal of Consulting Psychology*, 1968, *37*, 710–715.

Quinn, R. D. *Psychotherapists' expressions as an index to the quality of early therapeutic relationships.* Unpublished doctoral dissertation, University of Chicago, 1950.

Raimy, V. Phrenophobia and disabling anxiety. In A. R. Mahrer (Ed.), *The goals of psychotherapy.* New York: Meredith Publishing Company, 1967.

Rapaport, D. On the psychoanalytic theory of motivation. In M. R. Jones (Ed.),

Nebraska symposium on motivation. Lincoln: Univ. of Nebraska Press, 1960.

Redlich, F., & Hollingshead, A. *Social class and mental health.* New York: Wiley, 1958.

Rogers, C. R. *Client-centered therapy.* Boston: Houghton Mifflin, 1951.

Rogers, C. R. The necessary and sufficient conditions of therapeutic personality change. *Journal of Consulting Psychology,* 1957, *71,* 95–103.

Rogers, C. R. A theory of therapy, personality, and interpersonal relationships as developed in the client-centered framework. In S. Koch (Ed.), *Psychology: A study of a science.* (Vol. III, Formulations of the Person in the Social Context). New York: McGraw-Hill, 1959.

Rogers, C. R. *On becoming a person.* Boston: Houghton Mifflin, 1961.

Rogers, C. R. (Ed.). *The therapeutic relationship and its impact: A study of psychotherapy with schizophrenics.* Madison: Univ. of Wisconsin Press, 1967.

Rycroft, C. (Ed.). *Psychoanalysis observed.* Baltimore: Penguin, 1968.

Schofield, W. *Psychotherapy: The purchase of friendship.* Englewood Cliffs, N.J.: Prentice-Hall, 1964.

Shlien, J. M., Mosak, H. H., & Dreikurs, R. Effect of time limits: A comparison of two psychotherapies. *Journal of Counseling Psychology,* 1962, *9,* 31–34.

Sloane, R. B., Staples, F. R., Cristol, A. H., Yorkston, W. J., & Whipple, K. *Psychotherapy versus behavior therapy.* Cambridge: Harvard University Press, 1975.

Standal, S. C. A tribute to my teacher. *Voices: Journal of the American Academy of Psychotherapists,* 1975/76, *41,* 39–44.

Steinzor, B. *The healing partnership.* New York: Harper & Row, 1967.

Strupp, H. H., Wallach, J., & Wogan, M. Psychotherapy experience in retrospect: Questionnaire survey of former patients and their therapists. *Psychological Monographs,* 1964.

Szasz, T. The concept of transference. *International Journal of Psychoanalysis,* 1963, *44,* 432–443.

Truax, C. B., & Carkhuff, R. *Toward effective counseling and psychotherapy.* Chicago: Aldine, 1967 (book's quote states 1963).

Weiss, S. A. Therapeutic strategy to obviate suicide. *Psychotherapy: Theory, Research and Practice,* 1969, *6,* 39–42.

Wolpe, J., & Lazarus, A. A. *Behavior therapy techniques: A guide to the treatment of neurosis.* New York: Pergamon, 1966.

a
b
c
d
e
8 f
9 g
0 h
1 i
8 2 j